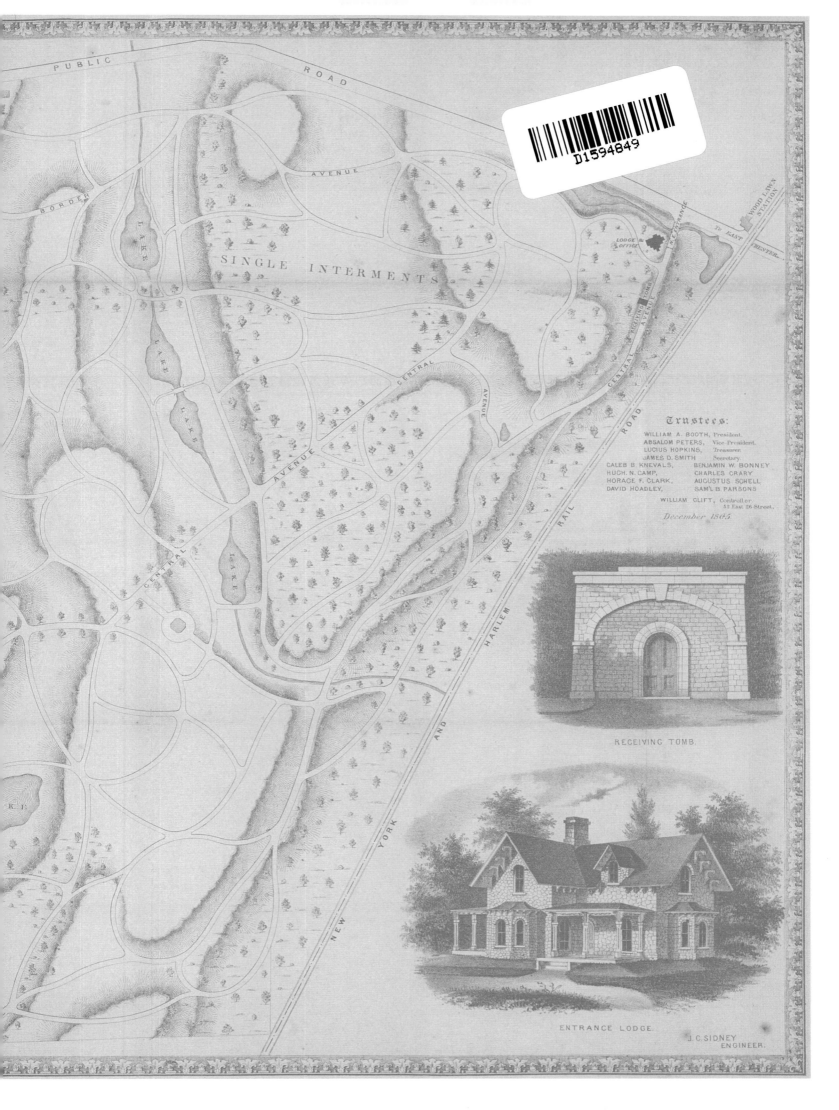

PUBLIC

ROAD

AVENUE

BORDER

SINGLE INTERMENTS

LAKE

LAKE

LAKE

CENTRAL

AVENUE

AVENUE

LAKE

AVENUE

CENTRAL

LAKE

WOOD LAWN STATION

To EAST CHESTER

LODGE & OFFICE

N. ENTRANCE

CENTRAL AVENUE

RECEIVING TOMB

ROAD

RAIL

HARLEM

AND

YORK

NEW

RECEIVING TOMB.

ENTRANCE LODGE.

J. C. SIDNEY
ENGINEER.

SYLVAN CEMETERY

ARCHITECTURE, ART & LANDSCAPE AT WOODLAWN

FRIENDS
BOYNTON BEACH CITY LIBRARY

In Memory of

MARJORIE WILKINS

Presented by

Lyn Slanetz,
Ruth C. Lindblad
Alice Abrams
Patrick Kelly
Peggy and Joseph Charny
Dr. David, Ann and Thomas Wilkins
Marcia Joslyn
Peter Sill

SYLVAN CEMETERY

ARCHITECTURE, ART & LANDSCAPE
AT WOODLAWN

*Edited by Charles D. Warren, Carole Ann Fabian
and Janet Parks*

AVERY ARCHITECTURAL & FINE ARTS LIBRARY
THE WOODLAWN CONSERVANCY

2014

Published on the occasion of the
Woodlawn Cemetery 150th anniversary exhibition held at
Miriam and Ira D. Wallach Art Gallery
Columbia University in the City of New York
September 3 – November 1, 2014

ISBN 978-0-692-24156-1

CONTENTS

ACKNOWLEDGMENTS

Cemeteries gain renown not only for the notables interred on their grounds, but also for their significant contributions to the development of the built environment in their locales. They become centers of vibrancy as parklands, places of memory, and repose. The Woodlawn Cemetery is additionally significant as a National Historic Landmark recognized for its development of the landscape-lawn plan which prompted the building of an unparalleled array of more than 1,300 mausoleums, exemplars of works by the most well-known architects, artists, and landscape designers in practice over Woodlawn's 150-year history.

In June 2006, Woodlawn Cemetery donated its expansive archive of historical records to the Avery Architectural & Fine Arts Library at Columbia University. Comprising approximately 900 linear feet, the archive includes architectural designs, maps, photographs, correspondence, construction and maintenance records, and other historical documents, spanning all the years of the cemetery's operations. Visitors to Woodlawn Cemetery experience the rich and diverse aesthetic of architects and designers whose works are gathered there in a verdant landscape. Researchers and students of architecture, urban planning, conservation technology, landscape design, art history and the decorative arts among other disciplines, view and study elements of the Woodlawn Cemetery archive at the Avery Library. Together, the archive and the Cemetery richly document works designed by the most prominent architects, landscape architects and artists, including: Carrère & Hastings; Daniel Chester French; Cass Gilbert; John LaFarge; Sir Edwin Lutyens; McKim, Mead & White; the Olmsted Brothers; John Russell Pope; James Renwick; Tiffany Studios; and Warren & Wetmore among many others. Taken together, The Woodlawn Cemetery, a place of inspiring beauty and cultural significance, and its archives at Avery Library present a rare and unique aesthetic, significant for its artistic and architectural merits, and now available for enjoyment and study by generations of scholars and the public.

Charles D. Warren, Susan Olsen and Janet Parks have provided the inspiration for every aspect of the Woodlawn projects. From facilitating the creation of the Woodlawn archive at Avery to conceptualizing the exhibition and book, their shared vision and insightful scholarship has guided our work, and their continuing dedication to all efforts have resulted in the production of this beautiful volume and engaging exhibition.

We are indebted to Gerald Beasley (former Director of the Avery Architectural & Fine Arts Library), Janet Parks, Susan Olsen and Charles D. Warren for recognizing the unique significance of this material and for their collective efforts to secure the Woodlawn legacy as a permanent archival record at Avery Library. Since acquiring the archive, Avery Library staff has worked on its processing and the publication of an online finding aid to facilitate research access to these extensive records. Special thanks must be given to Avery's archival staff past and present: Annemarie van Roessel, Leah Loscutoff and Shelley Hayreh who have led this effort, assisted by many Columbia University graduate students and interns, and to Jason Escalante (Drawings & Archives Assistant) for general assistance throughout the project.

Out of our archival work blossomed the *Sylvan Cemetery: Architecture, Art and Landscape at Woodlawn* exhibition and this accompanying volume – a celebration of the 150th anniversary of The Woodlawn Cemetery as well as the significant new partnership between Columbia and Woodlawn.

The exhibition *Sylvan Cemetery* marks the first time selections from the Woodlawn archive have been publicly displayed. Our dedicated curators – Janet Parks (Avery), Susan Olsen (Woodlawn) and Charles D. Warren – conceived the exhibition which surveys changing ideas about memorial monuments and commemorative landscapes since Woodlawn's creation in 1863. *Sylvan Cemetery* presents a carefully chosen selection of preparatory and design drawings, maps, building elevations, photographs, maintenance records, letters and books, placed alongside sculpture, metalwork, stained glass and other objects. In addition to selections from Woodlawn and Avery's collections, we are grateful to our lenders at the Bronx Borough President's Office, Topographical Bureau; Brookgreen Gardens; Connecticut Historical Society; Dr. Jovin Lombardo; Merriman Gatch; New-York Historical Society; Patricia Cronin Studio; Princeton University Library; The Metropolitan Museum of Art; University of California, Environmental Design Archives; University of Pennsylvania, Architectural Archives; Carolyn Schoonmaker; and Westerly Public Library & Wilcox Park. Their contributions help us offer a more complete picture.

The exhibition is produced in collaboration with The Miriam and Ira D. Wallach Art Gallery at Columbia University and its dedicated staff led by Deborah Cullen, Director and Chief Curator. We are grateful for the diligence, detail, and creativity of Jeanette Silverthorne, Associate Director of The Wallach Art Gallery, who has ably served as the project manager for the exhibition. Our special thanks to a skilled team of consultants, conservators, installation professionals, and archival staff for their guidance and assistance preparing and installing the exhibit: Alexis Hagadorn, Vasare Rastonis, Jennifer Jarvis (Columbia University Libraries' Conservation Lab). Last but certainly not least, we acknowledge the creative contributions of Ian Sullivan, our exhibition designer whose magic brought the *Sylvan Cemetery* to life for our broad public.

Charles Warren also served as lead author and editor of this accompanying volume. His extensive knowledge of Woodlawn from every perspective forms the intellectual construct for both the exhibition and this book. Mr. Warren and our three authors created essays that describe the creative development of the Cemetery: Charles Warren on landscape design, Andrew Dolkart on architecture, Alice Frelinghuysen on stained glass, and Cynthia Mills on sculpture. Collectively, their essays describe the unparalleled circle of creative work that makes Woodlawn a unique parkland of architectural and artistic achievement.

The editors and essay authors wish to thank Susan Olsen (Woodlawn Historian); the staff of the Avery Architectural & Fine Arts Library in particular Kitty Chibnik and Carolyn Yerkes; and the following for their contributors to the exhibit and publication: Merriman Gatch for generously sharing the Whiting family papers; Corinne Engelbert (Professor Dolkart's research assistant); Paris R. Baldacci (Professor Dolkart's husband and editor); the Columbia University Historic Preservation Program students who, since 2010, have used Woodlawn as a learning tool, completing the history and design analysis of many of the cemetery's mausoleums; and the Metropolitan Museum of Art staff members Kelly Mulrow (Administrative Assistant) and Christine Olson (Tiffany & Co. Foundation Intern).

The preparation of this book is the collective work of our creative and editorial teams. We thank Gavin Ashworth, Lee Sandstead, and Dwight Primiano for the exquisite photographic works included in this book. Jerry Kelly for the book design and production, who together with Kitty Chibnik, our text editor and indexer, attended to the myriad details of a cogently and beautifully presented volume.

The contributing scholars, book editors, and exhibition curators are thankful for the generous support of James G. Neal (University Librarian) and the Columbia University Libraries, The Miriam and Ira D. Wallach Art Gallery, the Board of Trustees of The Woodlawn Cemetery, the Board of Directors of the Woodlawn Conservancy and Woodlawn lot owners, foundations and business partners, all of whom have made this publication and exhibition possible.

Carole Ann Fabian
Director, Avery Architectural & Fine Arts Library

FOREWORD

When The Woodlawn Cemetery was established one hundred and fifty years ago, the founding Board of Trustees set out to build a "Rural Cemetery," a park like setting that would rival the established garden cemeteries of the east coast. Their vision for Woodlawn was to do more than provide an appropriate place for traditional memorialization and reflection; for this venture to be successful it was necessary to offer the latest in goods and services to accommodate the needs of sophisticated urban dwellers.

The earliest advertisements for the cemetery read "only thirty minutes from Manhattan," advising potential customers that you could get to Woodlawn easily by train. This modern convenience attracted attention and the cemetery began hosting "excursions" to bring notable New Yorkers out to the site. As the business endeavor began to take off, Woodlawn's Trustees embraced a new trend in cemetery planning. By adopting a new design style known as the Landscape-Lawn Plan, large open spaces with stately centerpiece memorials became the preferred way to commemorate the dead. By offering the latest in design, Woodlawn was distinguished from the other metropolitan burial grounds, providing the ideal setting for extraordinary Gilded Age monuments.

Woodlawn became fashionable. When the highly publicized construction of the Jay Gould mausoleum was completed in 1884, wealthy entrepreneurs of the time flocked to the cemetery to purchase sizeable lots. They commissioned the architects who built their estates to design their memorials. Alva Belmont, Robert and Ogden Goelet, Matthew C.D. Borden, Harris Fahnestock, Francis Garvan and William Whitney were among those who hired accomplished architects such as McKim, Mead & White, John Russell Pope, Peabody and Stearns, Carrère & Hastings and Hunt and Hunt to create their tombs. John LaFarge and Louis Comfort Tiffany crafted personal windows for their Woodlawn clients. Daniel Chester French, Sally James Farnham, Robert Aitken and Paul Wayland Bartlett were employed to sculpt figures that symbolized grief and morning in marble and bronze.

Newspapers, magazines and other publications featured articles on the famous cemetery. Titles such as *How the Rich are Buried*, depicted Woodlawn as a place where the wealthy could find peace. Reporters failed to acknowledge the commitment Woodlawn's Trustees had made to the community, to accommodate all races and cultures and to serve all the citizens of New York.

The Trustees supported efforts to connect the subway to Woodlawn, with the hopes of improving access to the cemetery and engaging a broader client base. By the dawn of the Jazz Age, Woodlawn was attracting a new clientele, leaders of the Harlem Renaissance, stars from the Broadway stage and the political leaders of the Progressive Era. Families brought the victims of the 1918 flu epidemic to the Bronx, and when fallen heroes were returned home after the First World War, they were honored at Woodlawn.

New designs were implemented to accommodate the thousands purchasing lots at Woodlawn after the Second World War. As families became smaller and spread across the nation, Woodlawn's leadership elected to develop spaces to suit the changing demographics and cultural trends. Community mausolea replaced private structures and smaller lots were designed to accommodate the new memorials manufactured by the modern machines employed by the monument industry. In recent times the cemetery invested in gardens and special spaces for the urns that are brought to Woodlawn today.

Throughout the years, Woodlawn's Trustees have dedicated their efforts to serving the needs of the community, ensuring the economic stability of the institution and honoring the memory of those in their care while maintaining a beautiful environment. And as the role of the cemetery in America changes once again, those involved in operating Woodlawn have become the stewards of an important green space, cultural resource, and internationally recognized historic site that attracts tens of thousands of visitors each year.

In 2006, the Board of Trustees of The Woodlawn Cemetery donated their archival collection to the Avery Architectural & Fine Arts Library at Columbia University. The decision to provide public access to this substantial collection of photographs, drawings, plans and correspondence illustrated the desire of the Woodlawn Board to promote the preservation of the collection of significant memorials and provide opportunities for scholars, students and family historians to gain a better understanding of memorial art, architecture and landscapes. By making these "private" records public, Woodlawn's collection of over 1,300 private family mausolea, hundreds of art glass windows and commissioned sculptures have been the subject of graduate studies, articles and restoration projects.

Through the efforts of curators, historians, interns and students studying the records and memorials a list of "significant features" was compiled attributing works found at Woodlawn to many celebrated artists, architects and landscape designers. When this roster was reviewed by the National Park Service in 2011, The Woodlawn Cemetery was designated a National Historic Landmark acknowledging that the site was "designed for convenient access to nearby New York City, it became a popular final resting place for the famous and powerful. Its memorials represent the largest and finest collection of funerary art in the country."

To commemorate these historic milestones, celebrated figures and the contributions of Woodlawn's Lot Owners, the Miriam and Ira D. Art Gallery at Columbia University presents the exhibition *Sylvan Cemetery: Architecture, Art and Landscape at Woodlawn.* The art and artifacts presented in the gallery and the collections on grounds of the historic site document 150 years of history and memory. The works selected by the exhibition's curators and contributing scholars inspire us to marvel at talent, discover the past and as a community serve as the stewards of a remarkable place.

GARDEN NECROPOLIS:
PLANNING WOODLAWN'S LANDSCAPE

CHARLES D. WARREN

WOODLAWN CEMETERY was founded in December 1863, a month after Lincoln so memorably dedicated the Soldiers' National Cemetery at Gettysburg, and a full generation after the first "rural" cemeteries were established in the 1830s. Its original plan included serpentine roads threaded through complex topography embellished by carefully tended plantings and edifying monuments. This type of picturesque cemetery landscape had become a recognizable American achievement.[1] But the Civil War altered attitudes towards death; new ideas about monuments, memorials, and cemetery design followed in its wake.[2] The city and the nation that emerged from this struggle – powered by steam, driven by shifting demographics, both enriched and corrupted by innovations in corporate capitalism – is mirrored in Woodlawn's architecture and landscape. Eventually, the cemetery's original "rural" character was overtaken by these forces of urbanism and Woodlawn was transformed.

French, British and German ideas contributed to Woodlawn's early development. The Parisian cemetery of Père Lachaise, which opened in 1804, is often cited as the inspiration for the "rural" cemetery movement, which first found expression in the United States with Mount Auburn Cemetery in Cambridge, Massachusetts (1831); Laurel Hill Cemetery in Philadelphia (1835); and Green-Wood Cemetery in Brooklyn (1838). But these American developments were also closely tied to those in Great Britain. Woodlawn's Congregationalist and Presbyterian founders had ecclesiastical and intellectual ties to Scottish and Nonconformist English culture, which made the Glasgow Necropolis (1833) and the suburban cemeteries of London of the 1830s and 1840s familiar and influential. By the time of Woodlawn's founding, British reformers such as John Strang and John Claudius Loudon had published books that served as guides to cemetery aesthetics and development. German ideas came later; within five years of Woodlawn's founding in 1863, Prussian-born landscape gardener Adolph Strauch's new cemetery style called the "landscape lawn plan" had an impact. Each new set of ideas and built examples affected Woodlawn's design.

By the end of the 1880s Woodlawn's designers had absorbed these influences and they began to synthesize a new style of cemetery landscape. They introduced large circular lots isolated by gravel paths, and in time, this planning innovation expanded beyond single focal points to become a flexible planning system. Circles were eventually deployed in groups stretching over varied topography. The monuments changed, too. Intricately carved, white marble statues, so popular in antebellum cemeteries, gave way to robust granite blocks, obelisks, and columns – these objects were larger, darker and more tightly integrated with their sites. Beginning in the 1880s, the elaborate mausole-

PLATE 1. J.M. Aertsen Darrach's domed Maclay mausoleum in Fairview plot in the foreground with the Hearn family's obelisk in the background. Photograph by Gavin Ashworth.

GARDEN NECROPOLIS   13

ums that are such a distinctive feature of Woodlawn's architecture grew in popularity and assumed a dominant place in the cemetery's landscape. From these innovations in the design of landscape and funerary monuments Woodlawn's unique character emerged (Fig. 1).

Between the Civil War and the Great Depression, Woodlawn underwent continuous development and change as America's most accomplished architects, sculptors, and landscape designers enjoyed the patronage of great fortunes. They vied with each other to memorialize individuals and dynasties with a funerary magnificence that drew inspiration from diverse, far-flung, architectural and garden antecedents. It was the cemetery's golden age of patronage and artistic quality. But now, a century and a half after the cemetery's founding, many individual landscapes of that era have changed beyond recognition. And though Woodlawn's architecture is largely intact, we struggle to reconstruct from photographs and drawings the full diversity and splendor of its landscape.

Woodlawn's eclecticism is not just an accumulation of sources. The diversity of architectural style threaded through its landscape reflects New York's culture and expresses attitudes about land

Fig.1. 1921 aerial view Woodlawn Cemetery by the Jerome Avenue gates. Avery Library, Drawings & Archives, Woodlawn Cemetery Records.

organization, real estate value, and social status, as much as it reveals religious, artistic, and symbolic aspirations. The sequence of landscape styles, the intentional, referential variety of the architecture, and the very shape of the land are expressions of changing ideas about death and memory, but they reveal something, too, about the life of the city.

Absalom Peters, the Founder of Woodlawn

Woodlawn was conceived by Reverend Absalom Peters in 1863 at the end of an active and controversial life as an evangelical entrepreneur. In 1837, Robert Breckinridge, a Presbyterian divine, wrote of him, "If ... Dr. Absalom Peters ...was desirous of revolutionizing this country, I know of no man but General [Andrew] Jackson who possesses more facilities to do it than he."[3] Peters was then head of the American Home Missionary Society (AHMS) and he controlled an educated army of young, zealous missionaries in the West. Through its journals, the *Home Missionary* and *Pastor's Journal*, which he edited, Peters had a direct means to communicate with growing congregations in western New York, Ohio, and the new states and territories further afield. He had a talent for raising funds from the prosperous merchants of New York, and Breckenridge was only one of many Presbyterian clergymen who saw the independence and power this gave him as a threat (Fig. 2).

Peters was born in New Hampshire in 1793 and he graduated from Dartmouth College in 1816. Three years later, after further study at Princeton Theological Seminary, he was licensed by the Presbytery of New York, and called to be pastor of a congregation in Bennington, Vermont. In 1823, he came to New York to lead the controversial AHMS. In the 1830s Peters became embroiled in controversial ecclesiastical trials, as squabbles over doctrine and church governance simmered. The banking crisis of 1837 further strained the church and helped make an intolerable irritant of AHMS and

Fig. 2. Absalom Peters. Born Wentworth, New Hampshire, September 19, 1793, died New York City, May 27, 1869. Portrait attributed to Frederick R. Spencer. Private collection.

other financially independent, voluntary societies not answerable to Presbyterian Church authority. The general Assembly of the Presbyterian Church passed a resolution "affirming that the organization and operation of the American Home Missionary Society ... and its branches of whatever name, are exceedingly injurious to the peace and purity of the Presbyterian Church. We recommend, therefore, that they cease to operate within any of our churches."[4] The independence of Peters and the AHMS from the authority of the church hierarchy was surely one cause of the schism into New School and Old School that followed.

At the end of 1837 Peters resigned as Corresponding Secretary of AHMS and launched two magazines *American Biblical Repository*, and the *American Eclectic*, which he co-edited. George Peters, his son, was enlisted as the publisher of these and a third magazine, the *American Agriculturist*. By 1842 both father and son had left these new ventures, but family connections to the *American Agriculturist* persisted. At about that time Peters helped found Union Theological Seminary, but his active involvement there was short-lived. In 1844 he was called to be pastor of the First Church of Williamstown, Massachusetts, and soon he became a trustee of Williams College. He lived in the relative placidity of Williamstown until returning to New York City in 1858.

Absalom Peters was part of New York's Benevolent Empire, a complex archipelago of philanthropy centered on the Broadway Tabernacle Church and the Third Presbytery of New York. Its islands were inhabited by abolitionists, sabbatarians, prohibitionists, Sunday school advocates, tract publishers, and evangelical missionaries of all kinds. Connecting them was a sea of belief in voluntary, cooperative action to spread the Christian gospel. These groups were funded in large measure by New York merchants, including Woodlawn founders William A. Booth, David Hoadley, Lucius Hopkins, and others. The sharp Yankee trading skills and Congregationalist traditions these New Englanders brought to the New York City in the decades after the Revolution transformed it. Their ideological zeal and religious orthodoxy chaffed against the pragmatic heterodoxy of New York, and their democratic patriotism contrasted with what remained of the Anglican aristocracy, which was seen by some of them as tainted by close association with the long British occupation.[5] To some extent Absalom Peters's Woodlawn project emerged from the decades of experience he shared with these immigrants to the city.

Peters had family connections in New York, too. His eldest brother, John R. Peters, was a wealthy cotton merchant and city alderman instrumental in transforming the potter's field between Waverly Place and West 4th Street into Washington Square Park. The value of John's real estate there was surely enhanced by the new park. The Reverend was no stranger to the business of real estate; he himself was a party to more than fifty property transactions in the five years between 1826 and 1839.

Peters's power had always derived from his ability to organize and raise money for evangelical projects. The American Home Missionary Society, Union Theological Seminary, and Williams College had all benefitted from his skill. The prosperous sons of New England, inspired by his combination of religion and activism, had generously heeded his call previously. Indeed, the reach of the Benevolent Empire relied on the grasp of New York's commerce.[6] At the end of his busy life, Peters used his skills and connections to advance one last project, but it was one that would benefit his heirs as well as the City of New York. Woodlawn was a complex real estate venture that mixed clerical propriety with potential profit and Peters was ideally prepared for it.

Founding Woodlawn

On December 23, 1863, Peters assembled a group of wealthy men at a bank in the village of Morrisania, a station stop on the New York & Harlem Railroad in what was then Westchester County. Several of these men were connected to the NY & Harlem, which months earlier had fallen into the hands of Cornelius Vanderbilt in a stunning stock market action known as the Harlem corner. With it came the rail route through Westchester County and along Fourth (now Park) Avenue to Madison Square in the center of the city and a monopoly on rail access to Manhattan. The rail line ran alongside the land Peters wanted to buy for his cemetery, just a few stops to the north. He needed investors and the NY & Harlem, a weakling of New York railroads, needed more passengers to make it profitable.[7] (Figs. 3, 4)

Fig. 3. New York & Harlem Railroad depot in background and New York, New Haven & Hartford Railroad depot in the foreground. Woodlawn maintained a city office in the vicinity of Madison Square from its founding until 1982. Cars were drawn by horses to 42nd Street where they switched to steam locomotives for the trip to Woodlawn. D.T. Valentine. *Illustrations for Valentine's Manuel* (New York, 1854-1867). Avery Library, Classics.

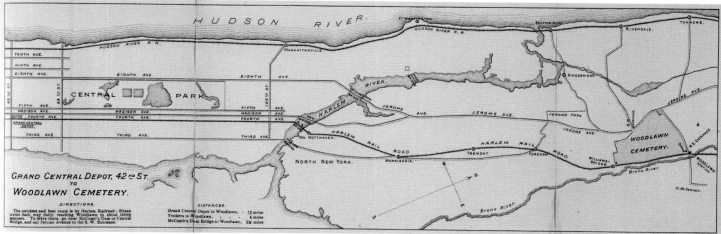

Fig.4. Early annual reports of Woodlawn Cemetery included this fold-out map of the train line from Grand Central to Woodlawn Cemetery. Avery Library, Drawings & Archives, Woodlawn Cemetery Records.

For Reverend Peters this meeting might have seemed like the last chance for his long contemplated cemetery; he could not let it slip through his shaky seventy-one-year old hands. The meeting details were recorded in the diary of John Jay Smith, the founder of Philadelphia's Laurel Hill Cemetery. As historian Aaron Wunsch has written, Smith was at the commercial center of the "rural" cemetery movement, advising cemetery founders and recommending designers for new "rural" cemeteries from Chicago to New York. Smith advertised his expertise with a book whose long title acknowledged its derivation: *Designs for Monuments and Mural Tablets: adapted to rural cemeteries, church yards, churches and chapels: with preliminary essay on the laying out, planting and managing of cemeteries and on the improvement of church yards. On the basis of Loudon's work.*[8]

Commenting on the difficulties Absalom Peters had encountered as he tried to organize a new cemetery, Smith wrote:

> The talking up of the project too often ended in the revocation of promises which had been made to [Peters]. By the time he had the assurance of one party, the previous one

Fig. 5. 1921 map recording land parcels assembled by Woodlawn Cemetery and The Woodlawn Associates. Avery Library, Drawings & Archives, Woodlawn Cemetery Records.

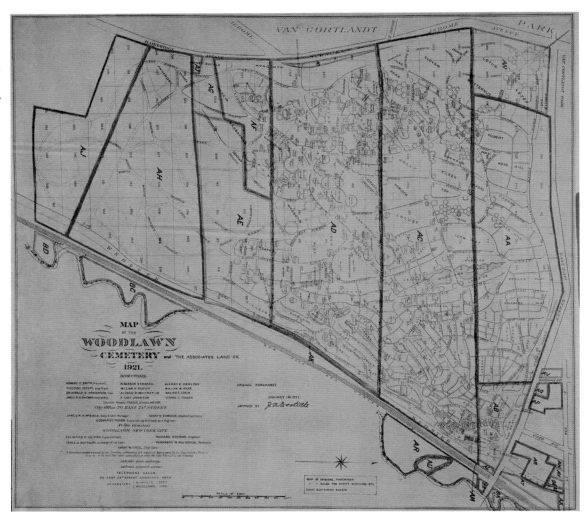

Key to 1923 Map showing the sequence of land acquisition by The Woodlawn Cemetery. Land was frrequently acquired by founders or trustees and then resold to Woodlawn.

Map	Seller	Sale Date	Buyer/Seller	Sale Date	Acres	Buyer
AA	Dr. Samuel Valentine	March 1, 1864	William A. Booth et al	May 31, 1864	58.51	Woodlawn Cemetery original land purchase
AB	Adam Spies	March 3, 1864	William A. Booth et al	May 31, 1864	89.00	
AC	Daniel Tier	March 28, 1864	Absalom Peters	May 31, 1864	100.00	
AD	Gilbert, John & Annie Valentine	April 12, 1864	Absalom Peters	May 31, 1864	91.77	
AE	Daniel Tier et al	March 28, 1864	Absalom Peters	May 31, 1864	32.72	
AF	William Valentine	March 31, 1864	William A. Booth et al	May 31, 1864	15.61	
AG	William Valentine	May 22, 1872	William A. Booth et al	May 1, 1874	3.592	Woodlawn Cemetery
AH	Anna L. Case	May 22, 1872	Hugh N. Camp	May 1, 1874	56.747	
AI	James Valentine	June 1 ,1875			0.49	
AJ	John Bussing	Jan. 1, 1879	J. Hugh Peters	March 18,1879	26.068	
AK	NY & Harlem Railroad	June 19,1889	J. Hugh Peters	July 2, 1889	1.162	
AL	NY & Harlem Railroad	Oct. 19, 1892			0.297	
AM	New York City	c.1896	Practically Abandoned		0.0373	
AN	Samuel H. Valentine	April 6, 1907			14.1764	
AO	New York City	Sept. 21, 1912			0.9886	
AP	George Opdyke	July 15,1873	Henry J. Diering	July 15, 1873	1.826	
AQ	George Opdyke	March 30, 1874			0.497	

Fig. 6. Key to 1921 map in Fig.5. Charles D. Warren.

had dropped his subscription. In despair he came to my house, and stayed long enough to study the subject and receive encouragement. I returned with him to New York. We visited the locality together, but lo! The period of refusal of the land had just expired. With difficulty we renewed, for a short time, this right to purchase.[9]

Smith recounted the meeting in Morrisania where:

Dr. Peters stated his plans and views, but there was evident coolness toward the project. With paper ready for subscriptions, a necessary assistance in such matters, I made a telling speech…I added that so satisfied was I that a new cemetery was a necessity that I came prepared to say the stock would be taken in Philadelphia, and that the scheme would proceed, but that I thought it would be more successful if it were a New York Project, and in the hands of the respectable gentlemen I saw around me. I handed out my subscription paper, signed my name for twenty thousand dollars of the small stock of one hundred twenty-five thousand dollars, and passed it round the table…It was nearly filled up, when one or two asked to double their original sums. The thing was done.[10] (Figs. 5, 6)

The NY & Harlem's interests were well-represented at the subscriber's meeting. Vanderbilt's son-in-law, Horace F. Clark, was accompanied by William Morris, the superintendent of the NY & Harlem and Augustus Schell, the Commodore's long-time ally. There were other railroad men present, too: David Hoadley, the canny president of the Panama Railroad and merchant Sheppard Gandy, soon to be a director of the Missouri Kansas and Texas Railroad and one of the original incorporators of the Metropolitan Railway Company (an unrealized NYC subway). There were merchants and bankers including James D. Smith, who later became president of the cemetery; Lucius Hopkins, Woodlawn's first treasurer; and Caleb B. Knevals, who later became the board's Vice-President.[11] William A. Booth, a banker and sugar merchant who served as president of Woodlawn's trustees, was there with his brother-in-law and business partner James A. Edgar. The group also included Westchester resident Hugh N. Camp, who had begun his career with Booth and Edgar, and two attorneys, Judge Benjamin W. Bonney and Charles Crary. Notable, too, in the party was the Quaker horticulturalist Samuel B. Parsons, owner of Flushing's most famous nursery.

There were many complex connections between Woodlawn's investors. Business interests such as cotton, sugar, banking, and railroads united most of them, but religious and cultural backgrounds were also shared. With the exception of Augustus Schell, the son of a German immigrant, Quaker Samuel Parsons, and Episcopalian Hugh Camp, all were members of Presbyterian or Congregationalist churches, several were descendants of prominent clergymen, and many were deeply involved in the Benevolent Empire. Most of them had been born in New England.[12] Philadelphian John Jay Smith was an outlier in the group, but after his important early role getting Woodlawn started, his participation faded.

Many "rural" cemeteries, such as Mount Auburn and Green-Wood were intended to operate on a not-for-profit basis once original investors had been repaid. But, as Smith made explicit, Woodlawn, like his own Laurel Hill, was intended to turn a profit. It conformed to New York State's Rural Cemetery Act of 1847, which allowed up to one half the sale price of each burial lot to be returned to investors. The other half was to be used for the development, operation, and maintenance of the cemetery. Woodlawn was a membership corporation, not a stock corporation; trustees were to be elected from the members (owners of burial lots.) This led to organizational complexity and some confusing terminology, but effective control of the cemetery rested in the hands of the investors and their heirs well into the twentieth century.

The original subscribers received shares proportional to their investments in an entity that over the years took various forms as a partnership and a corporation. Its name changed, too; sometimes called The Woodlawn Associates, The Associates Land Co., or just The Associates.[13] In exchange for the land this entity transferred to Woodlawn, the cemetery agreed to pay The Associates half the sale price of the lots as they were sold. The fact that William A. Booth was president of both the cemetery and The Associates for the first forty-three years and that all Woodlawn's trustees were also investors makes it difficult to disentangle Woodlawn Cemetery from The Associates. This problem was further complicated because The Associates owned other land surrounding the cemetery, but not officially connected to it. Operationally, the proportional interests of the investors were represented by, and traded like, stock certificates in Woodlawn, but care was taken to call it scrip or anything but stock. Starting in November, 1869, the cemetery paid regular (and handsome) sums to The Associates, which were distributed very much like a stock dividend.

Although Woodlawn was a non-denominational cemetery, as Green-Wood was, it had a marked Calvinist orientation. Large plots for the relocation of churchyard burials to Woodlawn were sold to Presbyterian and Dutch Reformed congregations, and, except for a few Episcopal ministers from Westchester, nearly all the many clergymen buried at Woodlawn came from Calvinist denominations. By contrast, Green-Wood's founders were predominantly Episcopalian.[14] Trinity Parish, the wealthy center of the Episcopal Church in New York, had considered buying a section of Green-Wood, but instead it established its own cemetery in Upper Manhattan's Carmanville in 1842. In the context of the ethnic tapestry that New York has become, the differences between these Protestant denominations appear minor, but doctrinal and historical differences between Episcopal and Calvinist churches were more powerfully felt in the nineteenth century. Antipathy between New York Anglicans and other Protestants lingered after the American Revolution, becoming a faint, but distinct echo that reverberated slightly with earlier struggles between the established Church of England and Nonconformists. A physical manifestation of these English divisions, Bunhill Fields Cemetery in London – sometimes called the Campo Santo of Nonconformists – provided historical sanction for unconsecrated, non-denominational cemeteries. These distant memories of tension between denominations were refreshed by the post-revolutionary influx of New Englanders into New York, which inform the differences between Woodlawn and Green-Wood. Religious orthodoxy, commercial sharpness, and new wealth were notable characteristics of the New England diaspora in New York; all were personified in Woodlawn's founders and influenced the cemetery's development.[15]

Just as Woodlawn's foundation was colored by denominational distinctions, its physical plan was predicated on a difference in geography and transportation that contrasted with Green-Wood in Brooklyn. Close ties to the NY & Harlem Railroad insured construction of a new station stop at Woodlawn's northern entrance. Funeral parties could board the horse cars at the rail depot north of

Madison Square and ride uptown to 42nd Street, where the cars were switched to a locomotive for the trip to Woodlawn and beyond. One reporter was struck by "the agreeable and easy access to the cemetery. No hot wearisome stretch of city distance, but a ride by car from 26th Street, through an avenue free from annoyance, speedily to find [oneself] in the cool, refreshing country."[16] Carriages making the journey from New York followed the route up Third Avenue and through Morrisania toward the Jerome Park Racetrack; Woodlawn's southern entrance was just a bit further up the road. Both of these routes allowed for a calm, dignified funeral procession in stark contrast to the trip to Green-Wood, which required mourners to suffer the traffic clogged streets of lower Manhattan and endure the jostling ferry ride across the East River. As the city grew, these difficulties became greater; the completion of the Brooklyn Bridge in 1883 failed to diminish Woodlawn's advantage because, by then, residential development and the churches that went with it had shifted uptown, making a funeral procession to Green-Wood even longer and a trip to Woodlawn even more convenient.

The railroad was key to Woodlawn's advantageous situation, especially after 1871 when Grand Central Depot opened. In 1875 the NY & Harlem built a funeral car called "Woodlawn" that could be hired for the journey. There were only a few such "railroad cemeteries." The largest and most notable of these was Brookwood Cemetery, also known as the London Necropolis, founded in 1849, and accessible via its own trains running between a private station adjacent to Waterloo and the cemetery. Woodlawn's 1864 annual report referred to another cemetery called Rosehill Cemetery in Chicago founded "about four years ago to be approached by steam cars in the manner we propose."[17] Early "rural" cemeteries such as Mount Auburn and Green-Wood were designed to be accessible by carriage. Railroad access made Woodlawn and Brookwood different: the journey was quicker, but still the train ride served to disconnect the "rural" from urban experience. In this, Woodlawn was similar to Olmsted and Vaux's residential suburb, Riverside, Illinois, and other planned, single purpose, park-like real estate ventures that were both convenient to, and sheltered from, the city. One was a garden city for the living, the other a garden city for the dead.

There was a utopian character to Woodlawn as there was to the American garden suburbs it resembled, but the idealism this implied was undercut by the commercial reality of land development. Peters had spent his early career nurturing religious outposts in the midst of newly plowed fields, and the railroad men who invested in Woodlawn understood that each whistle stop transformed the value of the land nearby.[18] Now they availed themselves of the opportunity to combine their experience to make a perfect and profitable cemetery. It had the sanction of their Nonconformist history, the leadership of a celebrated Presbyterian divine, and the corporate authority of New York State's Cemetery Act of 1847.

J.C. Sidney's "rural" Plan

The first plan for Woodlawn was drawn by James Charles Sidney in 1864 (Fig. 7). Sidney had worked for John Jay Smith at Laurel Hill, where he surveyed the grounds of the cemetery's southern addition in 1849. The 1854 lithograph Sidney printed with his partner P.W. Neff shows the plan he devised. His skill and connection to Smith led to other cemetery commissions along the Mahican channel from Montreal to Lansingburgh and down the Hudson to Woodlawn. Sidney was born

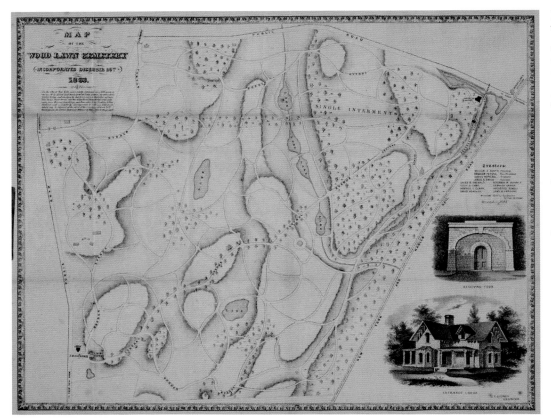

Fig. 7. The first published plan of Woodlawn, circa 1865. by James C. Sidney. The vignettes and title block were reused on subsequent maps, but their different size and border indicates the map was entirely new. The 1863 date refers to Woodlawn's founding, the date of the map is on the right side. Comparison with subsequent maps show how much of Sidney's road layout was changed. The absence of the 300-foot square grid, present on all subsequent maps, is notable. Avery Library, Drawings & Archives, Woodlawn Cemetery Records.

in 1819 and emigrated from England to Philadelphia. By 1845 he was working as a surveyor and draftsman for Smith. Most notable of his early accomplishments was the 1859 design of Fairmont Park in Philadelphia.[19] But Sidney had diverse talents and abilities; he drew plates for *Two Hundred Designs for Cottages and Villas*, a book by Smith and Thomas U. Walters; he authored *American Cottage and Village Architecture*; he published maps of Philadelphia and other cities; and he designed school buildings, estates, and hotels in Pennsylvania, New Jersey, and New York. His practice combined civil engineering with knowledge of "rural" architecture. In 1849 he published *Sidney's Map of Twelve Miles around New York with the Names of the Property Holders*, and, in 1851, a map of Westchester County. His local interests extended to a land development partnership at Spuyten Duyvil.[20] Sidney took on and shed a series of professional partners; Frederick Carles Merry collaborated with him from 1862-64 and worked on the buildings at Woodlawn, if not its plan.[21]

It is likely that Sidney was introduced to Woodlawn investors by John Jay Smith, but Charles Crary, another Woodlawn trustee, had also worked with him on an earlier cemetery project. Crary was trustee and treasurer of the Evergreen Cemetery Association in Salem, New York. He searched for its site, helped write its bylaws, and, along other town leaders, he hired Sidney to design the grounds of Evergreen Cemetery in 1859. It is a beautifully preserved example of Sidney's work.

Sidney's plan was the basis for the initial development of Woodlawn, and the cemetery prominently retains some of its features. Central Avenue, the cemetery's organizing spine, follows much of the route he established in 1864, and many of the roads in the northeast corner of Woodlawn still follow the routes Sidney traced. His hand can be recognized where the tight curves and steep, uneven grades of serpentine avenues are incised into the ground and bounded by gutters and sharply sloped turf margins. The plots defined by these roads have more closely spaced paths than those in the newer sections, and, although the hedges that once lined the perimeters of family lots have been removed, the few remaining iron fences make it possible to glimpse the landscape of Sidney's era.

Almost immediately Sidney's design was significantly altered by changes outside the cemetery gates. When the new road from McComb's Dam Bridge (Jerome Avenue) was built in the late 1860s, it followed a different route than Sidney had anticipated. This led to the relocation of the southern gate in 1871 and a major realignment of Woodlawn's Central Avenue (its original route is now Lin-

den Avenue) (Figs. 8, 9). Internal changes of equal significance included the re-grading of roads and the elimination of water features. With the exception of Woodlawn Lake, not one of Sidney's proposed water features is extant. The most notable loss is the "spring lake" that was once a visual focus near the intersection of Central and Ravine Avenues; such small, still ponds surrounded by hillside gravesites are a visual trope of the "rural" cemetery. When it was filled in and replaced by a fountain in 1872, the feature was diminished, but when its site was sold for the Vernon C. Brown mausoleum in 1920s, one of Sidney's most fully realized landscape

Fig. 8. Jerome Avenue Gate with bell tower, architect unknown (1871). Once the route of Jerome Avenue was established, Woodlawn built this new southern entrance where it intersected the cemetery perimeter. The gate was demolished and its bell was eventually reinstalled in the Woolworth Chapel. Avery Library, Drawings & Archives, Woodlawn Cemetery Records.

Fig. 9. Part of Frederick Law Olmsted's unexecuted plan for the "Central District" of the 23rd and 24th Wards of New York City. The land in southern Westchester County was annexed by the City in 1874; Woodlawn is at the bottom of the plan. It seems likely that the original southern gate to the cemetery was located with the mistaken assumption that Jerome Avenue (shown here as Central Avenue) would continue in a straight line from the intersection of Gun Hill Road, thereby terminating at Woodlawn's original southern gate. Bronx Borough President's Office.

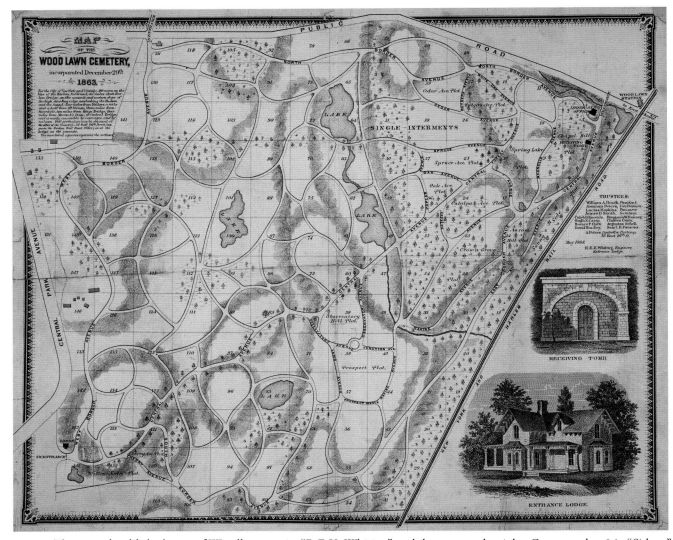

Fig. 10. The second published map of Woodlawn, 1868. "R.E.K. Whiting" and date are on the right. Compare the 1864 "Sidney" map. (Fig. 7) to see the alteration of roads and water features in the four years between these early maps. This map shows the 300-foot square grid that is the basis for Woodlawn cartography. Avery Library, Drawings & Archives, Woodlawn Cemetery Records.

features was erased. Harder to visualize is the series of streams, waterfalls, and ponds that once threaded through the cemetery's extreme north eastern corner and flowed under a bridge at its entrance. External road changes led to the abandonment of these features, and the water now flows through underground conduits, as it does where other water features, indicated in Sidney's plan, were abandoned or unbuilt (Fig. 10).

Early Days: Reverend William Avery Clift

Woodlawn's trustees were mindful of the need for someone to guide day-to-day operations including road construction and horticultural embellishment. After all, Sidney's plan was not much more than an arrangement of streets with a rather vaguely hachured suggestion of slopes and a sketchy indication of trees. They turned to Reverend William Avery Clift, Absalom Peters's son-in-law. Born in 1817, Clift graduated from Amherst College in 1839 and attended Union Theological Seminary while Peters was active there. A diary, which he kept at times in German, reveals a diligent student brought into the orbit of the Peters household while he was courting the Reverend's daughter Harriet.[22] He served as Pastor of the Congregational Church in Stonington, Connecticut, from 1844 until 1864 and wrote a regular column for the *American Agriculturist* under the pen name, Tim Bunker. This popular column, written in the homey vernacular of a Connecticut farmer, covered topics from Central Park's naturalism and the United States Sanitary Commission to the price of farmland. It reveals Clift's broad interest in scientific farming and horticulture.

Commenting on A.J. Downing's *Rural Essays,* Clift wrote in his diary: "choice – he was a unique genius."[23] Downing's magazine, the *Horticulturist,* which was edited by John Jay Smith after Downing's death, reflected the antebellum, anglophile tastes of the East Coast gentry. But the magazine Clift contributed to, the *American Agriculturist,* which reached a circulation of 100,000 by 1864, reflected the pragmatic outlook of its editors who came from the booming, prosperous farm land of western New York. It was aimed at the same audience Peters had evangelized with the American Home Missionary Society.[24] The quickly evolving scientific and mechanized farming methods promoted in its pages presaged a precise engineering of the land. Clift had imbibed Downing's antebellum aesthetic, but his own writing emphasized agricultural pragmatism and new technique more than "rural" taste.

Woodlawn's city office was at 52 East 26th Street, across from the depot of the NY & Harlem Railroad.[25] Clift rented the extra space there and moved his family to New York. He reported weekly to an Executive Committee of the trustees headed by William A. Booth and including Absalom Peters, Caleb B. Knevals, Charles Crary, James D. Smith, and Hugh N. Camp.

At the start of 1866, the Executive Committee's attention was occupied by land surveying methods and systems to identify lots and record sales. This led to a heated controversy, which changed the direction and leadership of the cemetery. At the Committee's January 17 meeting, Charles Crary, drawing on his experience at Evergreen Cemetery, proposed to divide Woodlawn into numbered sections defined by the curving avenues on Sidney's plan. Numbers 1 through 100 would run south to north on one side of Central Avenue and 101 through 200 would run the same direction on its opposite side. He proposed to omit a few numbers in these sequences for unanticipated changes. Peters objected and at the next meeting presented his dissent. He preferred to use a 300-foot square grid laid across the cemetery to identify and locate lots as had been done at Green-Wood (and as originally planned at Woodlawn). He said of Sidney's plan "The avenues and roads are already located by the practiced eye of Mr. Sidney, guided not by a previous survey, but simply by the lay of the land. But these of course are curvilinear and irregular, like the land itself. They bear no fixed proportionate relations to each other, and cannot be made the basis of measurement." He went on to characterize his own proposal:

> This is the plan on which our work has been begun after careful consideration of its scientific accuracy and convenience and of its practical working in the Green-Wood Cemetery: and I should greatly deprecate its supersedure by the random and unscientific plan proposed by Mr. Crary; which however practicable it may have been found in some Small Cemeteries, and even in large ones where a better plan had not been thought of, or duly considered, is utterly incapable of attaining the accuracy and perfections which characterize the Green-Wood Plan.[26]

Confronted with stark alternatives, strongly supported by Peters and Crary, the Executive Committee solicited an opinion from J.C. Sidney.

Sidney attended the February 14th meeting and expressed his opposition to Peters's plan (Peters objected to Sidney's views, too). At the next meeting it was voted to print one thousand copies of Sidney's plan with neither Peters's grid nor Crary's section numbers, thereby avoiding the contentious issue. Decisive action was finally taken on February 28th when the Executive Committee adopted Crary's system – Crary and Clift were charged with its implementation. At the next two meetings, with Peters absent, Charles Crary was made Treasurer of Woodlawn and put in charge of all affairs in the city office. Clift retained his title of Comptroller but was sent to take charge of the work on the cemetery grounds.

This gave Clift the opportunity to work more closely with Henry J. Diering, a German born and trained landscape gardener the cemetery had hired during its first year of operation. For nearly ten years Clift and Diering had lived in the same small Connecticut town; surely they knew each other well. In early spring they went on a spree, ordering a wide variety of new trees and shrubs from nurseries as far afield as their erstwhile home in Stonington. Some plants from the celebrated Flushing nursery of Samuel Parsons did not fare well and soon he left the board of trustees.

Crary took in hand the cemetery's finances and the matter of new roads planned by New York State around Woodlawn. Sidney's plan for a new cemetery section called Observatory Hill was approved at the June 6 Executive Committee meeting, but larger changes were foreshadowed when William A. Booth was asked to write to the "Cincinnati Cemetery" (Spring Grove Cemetery) requesting carte de visite views and there was a report of Clift's recent visit to Green-Wood. It seems likely that Peters could not reconcile himself to Crary's idiosyncratic plan for the numbering of lots. And although Sidney's design for another section of the cemetery was approved, the re-examination of Green-Wood's methods and the first sign of interest in Adolph Strauch's innovations at Spring Grove Cemetery indicated that dissatisfaction might extend beyond Crary's numbering system to include Sidney's plan itself.

On October 3, 1866, Crary resigned as Treasurer and two months later Clift told the Executive Committee he was leaving for a more congenial position as the assistant editor of the *American Agriculturist*. Absalom Peters was made Controller pro tem and quickly reasserted control over the development of the cemetery and its finances. He ordered new surveying instruments and moved furniture in the stone cottage so the surveyor, Mr. Burgess, could prepare a new map – presumably including a 300-foot grid. At the February 22, 1867 meeting, Booth was authorized to pay Sidney in full for the year 1866, evidently ending his employment at Woodlawn.

Robert Edward Kerr Whiting & the "lawn plan"

The cemetery was only three years old when Clift resigned, and, although Absalom Peters was remarkably energetic, he was seventy-three. Woodlawn needed a new Comptroller to develop its grounds and manage its business. On January 23, 1867, Woodlawn trustee David Hoadley wrote to William A. Booth introducing Robert Edward Kerr Whiting and recommending him to be Superintendant of Woodlawn.[27] Whiting was a resident of Hartford and an intrepid veteran of survey expeditions in Mexico and California. The year before, Hoadley had sent him to explore a potential railroad route connecting the Atlantic and Pacific oceans through the difficult tropical terrain of Colombia, a route that might compete with his Panama Railroad as Vanderbilt's Nicaraguan route had. Hoadley must have been relieved to learn the route was not viable for a railroad and impressed by Whiting's clear, thorough report.[28] (Fig. 11)

Fig. 11. Robert Edward Kerr Whiting, Born, New York, 1833; died, Lake George, New York, 1871). As Comptroller, Whiting was in charge of Woodlawn and its development from 1867 until his death. Private collection.

Peters hired Whiting for a trial period in April, 1867, and almost immediately, Whiting began producing reports for the trustees. On June 25 he addressed his first report to Peters concerning land sectioning and lot numbering. Without mentioning Crary's system, he explained the logic of the 300-foot square grid and the need for accuracy and consistency; he used Green-Wood as an example.[29] The grid controversy profoundly affected Woodlawn's development. It ended Sidney's influence and his method of "judging the lay of the land with a practiced eye."[30] Whiting replaced this method with increasingly precise surveying techniques. Henceforth, the 300-foot grid would appear on Woodlawn maps and Whiting's calculated elevations would make road grades gentle and constant.

The land might still be a canvas upon which the landscape artist could paint pictures, but money was at stake and precision was required. Sidney had preferred complex terrain laced with twisting roads of varying grades, as early "rural" cemetery designers generally did. But the deep swales on Sidney's road margins proved inconvenient to cross and inadequate to run-off from the steep ground. It was his misfortune that the first sections of the cemetery were on the steepest and most irregular terrain, and implementation of his plan proved difficult. Moreover, ideas about the landscape were changing along with everything else in postbellum America. New engineering techniques made it possible to shape the land to the needs of railroads, which required smooth, geometrically determined curves and gentle grades. Advances in hydrology and agricultural drainage methods made smoother road cross-sections possible, too, because ground water and surface run-off could be managed with subsurface drains rather than swales and gutters. The land was transformed from something to be judged by eye into something to be measured with instruments and then manipulated by men and machines.

By the end of the summer in 1867 Whiting had been hired permanently as the new Comptroller. In October he and Absalom Peters took a trip to Cincinnati to see the new style cemetery there and meet its cosmopolitan, Prussian-born landscape gardener Adolph Strauch. Spring Grove Cemetery, as it was called, was originally designed as a "rural" cemetery, but starting in 1855, it had been transformed by Strauch. Whiting relates Strauch's description of Spring Grove's early history: "The first ten years of which were passed in carting <u>in</u> stone and iron … he has been engaged in the last ten years in carting it <u>out</u>" then commented, "evidence of the truth of which we saw in the piles of condemned

Fig. 12. An aerial view of Spring Grove cemetery in Cincinnati illustrates the conception of the landscape at the largest scale. The sweeping entrance drive leads to the cemetery grounds embellished with large monuments and undivided by fences. Courtesy of Spring Grove Cemetery.

Fig. 13. Narrow path between Macy and Colgate lots in Magnolia plot in Woodlawn Cemetery. In early plots, iron and stone enclosures divide the landscape and usually follow lot borders. In this view the enclosure follows the path rather than the circular shape of the Colgate lot. Photograph by Gavin Ashworth.

iron fences, rails and stone posts lying ready for removal."[31] A.J. Downing had also ridiculed the "ironmongery" that spoiled American cemetery landscapes, but Strauch had designed and enforced an alternative. He called it the "landscape lawn plan." (Figs. 12, 13)

The new style sought a sweeping, continuous, naturalistic landscape without fences or the clutter of varied, multiple headstones and mounds marking individual burial locations. Instead of a patchwork of small, fenced lots crowded with many individual monuments, Strauch proposed a more communal landscape featuring horticultural, topographic, and artistic embellishments united by broad continuous lawns. Lot owners were restricted to one monument with only low stones marking gravesites and property boundaries. Reporting on the visit, Whiting wrote, "Mr. Strauch's idea is that roads should sweep in long and graceful curves, totally avoiding the abrupt twists and turns that disfigure Green-Wood and the cemeteries that have adopted it as a model – that they should be broad ... – that the grade should never exceed one foot in fifty thereby avoiding the use of gutters and finally to use his own language 'the fewer roads the better.'" One sentence of the report points to Whiting's familiarity with recent cemetery developments: "I called the attention of Mr. Strauch to the iron caps used to mark lot corners at Cedar Hill Cemetery near Hartford by Mr. Weidenmann, who was formerly engaged upon Spring Grove Cemetery."[32]

Whiting knew of the "lawn plan" prior to the Cincinnati trip because of his connections to Hartford's Cedar Hill Cemetery, which was designed on the "lawn plan" in 1864 by Strauch's colleague, the Swiss-born landscape gardener, Jacob Weidenmann.[33] Cedar Hill connections also brought Whiting in contact with James Good-

Fig. 14. Monument to General William Jenkins Worth (1856), Fifth Avenue and 24th Street looking east across Madison Square Park. This monument is the burial site of General Worth and the first major project of James G. Batterson in New York City. Avery Library, Classics.

Fig. 15. Samuel Colt Monument, Cedar Hill Cemetery, Hartford, Connecticut. Designed by James G. Batterson with a bronze figure by Randolph Rogers. This Egyptian Revival monument with small grave markers in the foreground exemplifies the "Landscape Lawn" idea of prominent artistic monuments surrounded by a continuous lawn. Small Celtic cross is a later addition. Charles D. Warren.

win Batterson, one of that cemetery's founders, who guided its development as a trustee for more than forty years. Batterson was an innovator in granite quarrying, steam-powered stone working, and monument design and he worked closely with those at the forefront of cemetery landscape design. His 1857 monument to General William Jenkins Worth just west of Madison Square brought him to prominence in New York, and he remained at the center of cemetery and memorial design throughout the second half of the nineteenth century.[34] (Fig. 14) Whiting's familiarity with Batterson and the "lawn plan" had far-reaching consequences for Woodlawn (Fig. 15).

Appended at the end of the Spring Grove report is a note signed by Absalom Peters saying, in part "it affords me pleasure to add my Entire Approval of the preceding report."[35] Cautiously, Woodlawn's trustees decided to experiment with the "lawn plan." Whiting designed a scheme for Prospect and Observatory plots in an area of the cemetery separated from the "rural" sections by existing woodlands. A diagram showing the preferred "lawn plan" lot configuration and other rules were added to the annual report in 1868 (Figs. 16, 17). The numbering sequence of lots in these two plots differed from earlier practice, too – it was determined by location rather than order of sale.

Peters's approval of the "lawn plan" experiment eased adoption of its tenets, but already established "rural" sections of the cemetery were kept under the old rules and sales there continued; Woodlawn wanted it both ways. At the close of 1868, cemetery development was expanding south across the grounds and its management by Whiting and Peters was a success. But by the beginning of 1869, Absalom Peters's health was declining and he died on May 18, 1869. By then the cemetery, which he founded was taking shape. Peters was buried in the lot numbered "one." The place was marked with a granite obelisk overlooking Spring Lake and the Bronx River valley beyond.

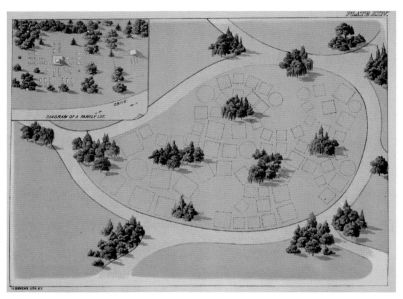

Fig. 16. Cedar Hill Cemetery, Hartford, Connecticut, designed by Jacob Weidenmann. Main illustration shows the layout of a plot into individual lots following "Landscape Lawn" principles. Note the large open area, between lots, that was not for sale. The inset shows a lot in detail with a prominent central monument and unobtrusive individual grave markers. Jacob Weidenmann. *Modern Cemeteries* (Chicago: Monumental News, 1888). Avery Library, Classics.

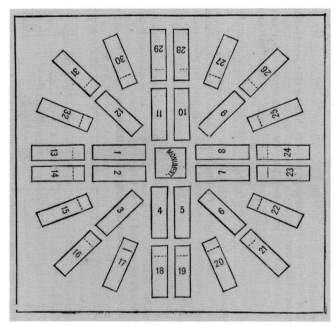

Fig. 17. Landscape Lawn Plan diagram from Woodlawn annual report. Note the similarity to the Weidenmann lot diagram (Fig. 16). Avery Library, Drawings & Archives, Woodlawn Cemetery Records.

Civic & Sepulchral Monuments: Farragut, Batterson & Saunders

In 1870 Woodlawn gave the widow of Admiral David Glasgow Farragut a prominent burial lot at the center of Aurora Hill plot overlooking the Bronx River. Farragut was a Civil War hero and this gift honored his memory as it brought honor to the cemetery, but this memorial introduced an aspect of civic commemoration into the midst of a private cemetery. Though the monument was well within cemetery norms, the lot's distinctive circular plan set it apart. The contoured turf surface of this circle rose smoothly towards the center like a lens or a low saucer dome. Its 247-foot circumference was defined by a gravel path. This binding and shaping of the land proclaimed its separateness and civic importance. It is the first time these features appear at Woodlawn (Figs. 18, 19) (see Fig. 95).

Such lens-shaped circular lots were not unknown in the naturalistic "rural" style that Woodlawn and other cemeteries had followed, but they were usually interspersed among the more usual rectangles and bounded by iron fences rather than gravel paths. Nehemiah Cleaveland's earliest book on "rural" cemeteries illustrated examples of these at Green-Wood, and notably the plot owned by

Fig. 18. Admiral David Glasgow Farragut lot in Aurora Hill plot. Though earlier lots were described as circles on the map, this is the first to be mounded in the shape of a low dome with a gravel path describing its circumference. Photograph by Gavin Ashworth.

the eldest brother of Absalom Peters there was also round (Fig. 20). These mounded circles may derive from ancient traditions of burial mounds and tumuli, but in the context of the "rural" style, they can appear as artificial anomalies that contradict a carefully cultivated naturalism.[36] This is more evident now when so many of the fences that once visually anchored the circles have been removed (Fig. 21).

The taste of Farragut's widow and son were expressed in their choice of an intricately carved, white marble monument that is almost at sea on the large swelling lawn. We have no record that Whiting advised her, but we know he was involved in the selection of other monuments. In a letter to his wife, he fretted over the nearby hillside mausoleum of Thomas P. Eldridge and then wrote about another monument: "The owner of a large lot on the Lawn Plan ... wants to go to Hartford with me to see Batterson's works. He manifests a disposition to stick by me until I can pick out a monu-

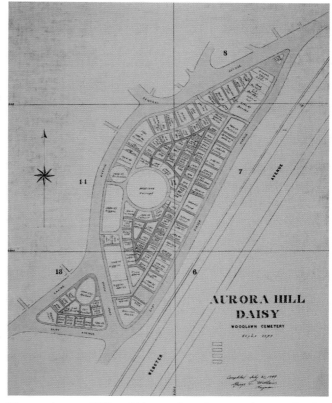

Fig. 19. Aurora Hill and Daisy plots showing the circular Farragut lot and its circumferential path. Avery Library, Drawings & Archives, Woodlawn Cemetery Records.

ment."[37] It is surprising that Batterson was not commissioned for the Farragut monument, if only because of the prominence of his Worth monument. But the striking similarity of the Farragut lot to gravel-edged, lens-shaped lawns Batterson used to anchor monuments in town green projects such as

Fig. 20. An example of a mounded circle at Green-Wood Cemetery. Note that it is defined by a fence and appears as the top of a natural hillock. Nehemiah Cleaveland. *Green-Wood Illustrated* (New York: R. Martin, 1847). Avery Library, Classics.

Fig. 21. Green-Wood Cemetery in Brooklyn had circle lots, but they were defined by fences (if at all) and not paths. Lot number 9925 belonged to John Peters, the brother of Absalom Peters, Woodlawn's founder. Courtesy of the Green-Wood Cemetery.

the one in East Bloomfield, New York, suggests that such civic memorials influenced developments at Woodlawn (Fig. 22).

Farragut's lot design drew on other better known examples, too. At the Soldiers' National Cemetery in Gettysburg, designed by William Saunders, the contoured circle is a prominent feature. There, a Batterson monument (George Keller was the architect, the sculpture was by Randolph Rogers) occupies the center of a partial circle surrounded by concentric arcs of small, low, identical grave markers – it is a "lawn plan" lot on a civic scale (Figs. 23, 24). The circle's edge is undefined, so nothing distracts or interrupts the continuous carpet of turf as it swells up from a natural hill to form a symmetrical mound. The granite monument crowns this landform as it gathers up the

Fig. 22. Civil War monument in East Bloomfield, New York, (1868) by James G. Batterson. Note the mounded earth form defined by an encircling path. Batterson's New England Granite works was one of the major designers of Civil War-era monuments. East Bloomfield Historical Society.

land's forces. Together they suggest that expressive artifice can shape the land as it had long been used to sculpt stone, and that land and monument can be fused in a single composition. This form of landscape monumentality is very different from the "rural" cemetery's juxtaposition of object and landscape; its influence at Woodlawn extended far beyond the mounded form of the Farragut circle.

Woodlawn is fenced and sepulchral as the Gettysburg cemetery was, but as a private landscape it is an uneasy place for a truly civic monument. This was illustrated when Augustus Saint-Gaudens won the commission for a second monument to Farragut in Madison Square; evidently the need was felt for a prominent memorial in a civic location. Similar tensions between cemetery and civic monuments had been made explicit when the DeWitt Clinton Monument Association decided his monument should have a civic rather than a sepulchral character. Turning aside many offers of cemetery sites, they chose a place in the center of Albany and proposed a triumphal arch design by James Renwick Jr. The Committee hoped that Clinton would be buried beneath his monument, but the Governor's family declined to move his remains from Green-Wood. Eventually a bronze statue, commissioned from Henry Kirke Brown, was given a short "civic" display in City Hall Park before being moved to Green-Wood, a location that gave it a decidedly sepulchral character after all.[38] (Fig. 25)

Historian Blanche Linden has written about early nineteenth-century cemetery monuments as edifying reminders of public and private virtue.[39] But they had another purpose in some cemetery contexts and that was to lend the sanction of great reputations to nearby ground that was, after all, for sale. Farragut's reputation enhanced Woodlawn's as Clinton's had Green-Wood's. The number of heroes and statesmen in these suburban cemeteries increased as Manhattan churchyard cemeteries were vacated for new development, but the need for reminders of civic virtue in the city center persisted. Madison Square contained New York City's greatest concentration of memorials beginning with the Worth monument and followed

Fig. 23. Soldiers' National Cemetery at Gettysburg, the battlefield cemetery dedicated by Lincoln with his famous address. Landscape designed by William Saunders, with monument by James G. Batterson and sculpture by Randolph Rogers. This "Landscape Lawn" style monument is at the top of a lens-shaped mound and at the center of concentric semi-circles described by low markers for individual graves.

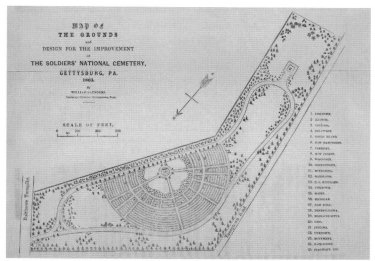

Fig. 24. William Saunders's 1863 plan for Soldiers' National Cemetery at Gettysburg. Columbia University Libraries.

by others for Chester A. Arthur, William Seward, Roscoe Conkling and Saint-Gaudens's celebrated Farragut. Worth's remains were buried under his monument, but the unity of sepulchral and civic locations became increasingly unusual, in part because burials south of 86th Street were forbidden after 1851. Woodlawn, like other "rural" cemeteries provided a separate, specialized landscape that removed this aspect of civic memory from the city's center and concentrated it in a single-purpose suburb.

The combination of monuments and circular lots at Woodlawn was surely influenced by boulevard terminations in Haussmann's Paris or Olmsted and Vaux's Buffalo. But James G. Batterson was pivotal in adapting these forms to the cemetery landscape. After Farragut's lot, other large, circular lots at Woodlawn such as Low/Harriman and Havemeyer followed the pattern it created; each had a tall monument at the center of a defined circular perimeter. Most of these monuments came from Batterson's New England Granite works and some were accompanied by raised, circular, granite

curbs from the same source. His artistic interest in monument design, his commercial interest in quarries and steam-driven lathes, and his familiarity with the "lawn plan" positioned him to devise or at least influence a fusion between monuments and their landscapes (Fig. 26). Batterson helped define the style of Woodlawn's memorials and landscape well into the 1890s. But as these combined landscape/monument forms were transformed into pliable design devises, they lost some of their civic associations and came to represent wealth, taste, or the assertion of prominence, but not necessarily public virtue.

Early Mausoleums

Woodlawn's first hillside tomb was constructed for the Addison Jerome family in 1866, just across Ravine Avenue from Farragut's circle. Its single exposed façade gives access to what was otherwise an underground vault. Similar hillside tombs were located along Ravine Avenue as it climbed steadily up the side of the valley following Whiting's carefully calculated grades. There is another row of hillside tombs on East Border Avenue, but changes in style and advances in embalming techniques made the cool, constant temperature of these underground vaults less critical.[40] By the late 1870s the construction of aboveground structures such as the Classical-style Butterfield mausoleum began to alter Woodlawn's appearance. By 1880, a mausoleum was combined with a circular lot for the first time in the tomb of Marshall Roberts. It had both a gravel path and a raised circle of granite curbing to emphasize its distinctive perimeter. This began a new

Fig. 25. DeWitt Clinton Monument, Albany, New York, by James Renwick, 1848 (unbuilt). Intended as a public monument near the New York State Capitol (seen in the background) where it was proposed Clinton would be buried. Clinton Monument Association, *The Clinton Monument MDCCCXLVIII* (New York: Van Norden, 1848). Pennsylvania. General Assembly. House of Representatives. Select Committee Relative to the Soldiers' National Cemetery. *Revised report of the Select Committee Relative to the Soldiers' National Cemetery.* (Harrisburg: Singerly & Myers, State Printers, 1865).Columbia University Libraries.

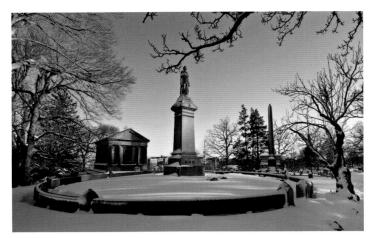

Fig. 26. James Low/Oliver Harriman monument in Magnolia plot with the Huntington mausoleum in the background. The curved granite curb anchors the lens-shaped landform in a section of the cemetery where fences or hedges once separated most lots. The monument is characteristic of James G. Batterson's New England Granite Co. at this time. Photograph by Gavin Ashworth.

Fig. 27. Marshall O. Roberts mausoleum, circa 1880, in Crown Grove plot, the first mausoleum built in a circular lot. Photograph by Gavin Ashworth.

phase of cemetery development that combined specific architectural style (in this case, Gothic) with a circular lot that began to establish Woodlawn's increasingly distinctive character (Fig. 27).

Whiting's reports continued to explain the aesthetic benefits of the "lawn plan," and when he demonstrated that the new plan yielded more saleable land, this economic rationale was persuasive for some trustees. By March 1871, Charles Crary had been won over; he wrote: "I like especially … where you speak of the Landscape Lawn Plan …We certainly are indebted to you for the good correctness and persistence with which you have advocated that plan."[41] On a visit to Laurel Hill in October, 1870, Whiting was startled when the Quaker John Jay Smith addressed him with "thee" and "thou." Whiting compared the Philadelphia cemetery unfavorably with Hartford's Cedar Hill, specifically mentioning the "curious foreign trees." As if intentionally closing the book on the influence of Smith and Laurel Hill, he commented, "it not only possesses no merit but is positively forbidding."[42]

A recurring illness had plagued Whiting since his days in Mexico and it worsened as the birth of his second child approached. He left his wife in the care of her mother and went away to recover his health. After a few idle days in Saratoga, he arrived at the Lake George Hotel on September 9 where he died the next day.[43] Robert E.K. Whiting transformed Woodlawn from an imprecise plan that existed mostly on paper to a prosperous and well-managed cemetery. He influenced Woodlawn's physical development by helping introduce the "lawn plan" and persuading the trustees to adopt some of its tenets; he provided leadership and took charge of the cemetery's business affairs; he began more systematic surveying and planning that altered the design of the cemetery and the arrangement of its avenues; and he introduced James G. Batterson, whose influence altered the appearance of Woodlawn's monuments and its landscape. It was under Whiting that the first circular lots were built. In less than five years he remade Woodlawn.

Circles of Sepulcher: Knevals, Diering, Griswold

Replacing Whiting was impossible, so his responsibilities were divided. Trustee Caleb Knevals was given charge of overall management as Comptroller in the city office, and, on the cemetery grounds, landscape gardener Henry J. Diering was promoted to Superintendent and assisted by a newly hired engineer named Charles Griswold.

Knevals was one of the founders of Woodlawn and a member of the board's Executive Committee; he was a merchant in the sugar importing firm Wylie, Knevals & Co. and his family ties to other Woodlawn founders were complemented by his involvement with evangelical philanthropies of the Benevolent Empire. In 1869-70 he was caught in a bribery scandal at the Customs House. As Knevals immersed himself in the cemetery's affairs, there is no sign that Woodlawn's trustees were troubled by his combination of philanthropic propriety and graft.[44] In 1874 the Executive Committee acknowledged his hard work by paying him an extra $1,500 over his salary of $9,000 (three times the salary they had paid Whiting). By February 1878, the firm Wylie, Knevals & Co. was bankrupt, leaving him more dependent on his Woodlawn income and with more time to devote to the cemetery.

Perhaps Charles Woodward Griswold was being considered to help with a topographic survey of the cemetery prior to Whiting's death, because little time elapsed between that event and Griswold's

Fig. 28. Woodlawn's first contour map by Charles Griswold, 1874. Griswold used the plane table technique to make this survey. The map and its southern extension, made the following year, was used and updated until the end of the nineteenth century. Avery Library, Drawings & Archives, Woodlawn Cemetery Records.

arrival in October 1871. He had graduated that year from Yale's Sheffield Scientific School. Soon after his arrival Griswold wrote three detailed reports: one on site hydrology and drainage; a second on the geometry and configuration of lots; and a third advocating the production of a detailed contour map. These reports had far-reaching consequences in Woodlawn's development. The two maps he completed in 1875-76 provided the first complete topographic view of the cemetery. Their precisely surveyed contour lines integrated earlier measurements and replaced the hachuring that Sidney had used to vaguely illustrate landforms. These maps recorded and guided changes to the land for the next twenty years (Fig. 28).

Griswold's report on hydrology set out the requirements for the proposed lake and explained the need for agricultural tiles to drain swampy land at its perimeter. By the 1880s, use of these tubular ceramic tiles had become widespread on American farms, producing dramatically better yields and profits. At Woodlawn, burial requirements necessitated their placement eight feet below the ground rather than the two feet used on farms, but they served the same ends – making land usable and profitable. Without the drain tiles, the land around the lake was too wet for burial purposes and the water they collected helped supply the lake (Fig. 29).

Griswold's report on the geometry and economy of lot design was an advance on earlier reports by Whiting. In it he makes the distinction between cemetery "plots," which are large sections defined by avenues, and the "lots," into which they were divided for sale. He calculated the most economical shape or figure to be used as a boundary and explained: "Calculus proves this [most economical] figure to be a circle … but we have to consider a large group of plots and as circles cannot be grouped without great loss, it is not the best form." Using the recently developed Beech plot to advance the argument against circle plots, he calculated the sale price of land including the waste factors due to roads, margins, and paths. Griswold asserted that Woodlawn's high land value makes it worth "overcoming obstacles" (by which he meant natural features) to create rectilinear plots, concluding that plots should be "just as large as we can sell and as nearly square as the configuration of the ground and principles of aesthetics will permit." Griswold was arguing against circular plots, but his calculations tell a different tale about circular lots. He explained that the average sale price per gross foot in Beech plot was $1.03 while the circular Havemeyer lot at its center sold for a price of $1.57 per gross foot. The fact that Havemeyer is an internal lot (one not bordering an Avenue) makes his comparison even more dramatic because internal lots realized only $0.88 per gross square foot. Plainly, though Griswold does not draw this conclusion, laying out a large circular lot at the center of a plot allowed the cemetery to charge a higher price for otherwise less valuable land. The analytical tone of this report is striking. It illustrates how economic calculation and engineering technique were transforming, or at least, influencing the design of Woodlawn's landscape. [45]

The Havemeyer lot was important in the evolution of the circular lot at Woodlawn, and not only because the family paid a premium for it. William F. Havemeyer was not a war hero like Farragut, but he did represent a kind of civic virtue; he was an anti-Tweed reformer and the first New York mayor since DeWitt Clinton to have held that office three separate times. The large, prominent lot, so similar in design to the Civil War monuments Batterson had recently completed, followed the pattern of Farragut: a private sepulchral monument given civic prominence by its circular site design.[46] (Fig. 30) (see Fig. 97)

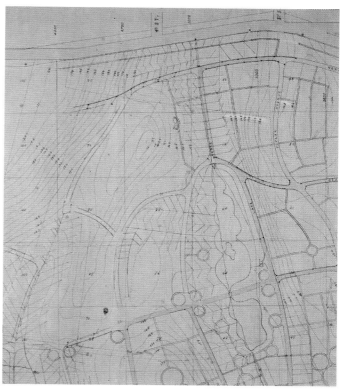

Fig. 29. 1874 Griswold map detail showing the arrangement of subterranean drain tiles in red. Use of these tiles made wet low-lying land usable for burials. Avery Library, Drawings & Archives, Woodlawn Cemetery Records.

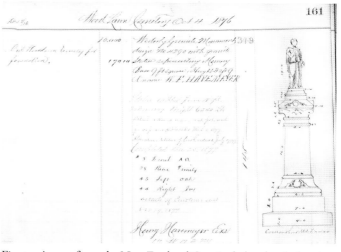

Fig. 30. A page from the New England Granite ledger book showing a sketch a figure atop a pedestal, by Carl Conrads, that was placed at the center of the Havemeyer lot in Beech plot. Courtesy of the Westerly Public Library.

Griswold's engineering methods were more up-to-date than Whiting's; his analysis of drainage and plot configuration altered future planning, and many of the recommendations in the reports he produced were adopted. After 1880 plots were made larger and more nearly square, and, in 1884-87,

Woodlawn Lake was constructed using methods he suggested. But he was an engineer, and, unlike Whiting, he was subordinate to Henry J. Diering, who had been appointed Superintendant and Landscape Gardener. Slowly, Diering had come to control the design of the cemetery as much as any individual did. Griswold had married and started a family at Woodlawn, but he had health problems. A little over six years after his arrival he developed "an acute mania" attributed to over-work. Griswold died in a Poughkeepsie asylum on February 3, 1878 at the age of 25.

Henry J. Diering

In its first fifteen years Woodlawn had four Comptrollers – Clift, Peters, Whiting, and Knevals and three engineers – Sidney, Whiting, and Griswold. All the while, the remarkable, German-born landscape gardener Henry J. Diering had supervised the work of grading and planting. When he was made Superintendant of Woodlawn in 1872, his control was consolidated and his importance confirmed. Diering was born in 1828 at Sultzburg in Baden where he received an education until the age of fourteen. He then began an apprenticeship in Freiburg typical of the German system. J.C. Loudon described this practice:

> The term of apprenticeship is three years and a half, and for travel three years….When [the apprenticeship] is completed, the youth is initiated into what may be called the free-masonry of gardening, and being furnished with a password, he proceeds from one town to another, till he can get work … In this way he may walk over the whole of the German empire, Denmark and part of Holland.[47]

The details of Diering's travels are unknown, but his extended education lasted until 1849 when he was drafted into the army. In 1851 he emigrated to the United States and found work as a gardener in Flushing and then Yonkers. He went to New Orleans in 1853 and, after a year and a half, he returned north and settled in Stonington, Connecticut, where he lived from 1855 until he moved to Woodlawn in 1864.[48] He shared the native language and, to a degree, the cosmopolitan background of Adolph Strauch and Jacob Weidenmann.

In August, 1872, Knevals and Diering took a study trip to visit Adolph Strauch at Spring Grove, following the earlier example of Peters and Whiting. It must have refreshed the influence of the "lawn plan" for Woodlawn's new leadership. Woodlawn's meeting minutes mentioned their stop in Philadelphia on the way home, reporting: "from Laurel Hill, they had nothing to learn."[49]

Diering's role grew steadily from experienced landscape gardener to mastermind of Woodlawn's artistic landscape. At first, he may have needed Clift's conversant German and smooth clerical manners and surely he relied on the engineering skills of Whiting and Griswold, but these men were amateurs in horticulture and landscape design, a field in which Diering had both training and experience. After Griswold's death, Judson Doolittle, another Sheffield Scientific School trained engineer, was hired to replace him, but he was subordinate to Diering and many years his junior. A later trustee, Charles H. Edgar, was partially correct when he said of Henry Diering "He simpl[y] laid out lots in a way he thought best without any preliminary survey, and I have heard him say that if people did not want the lot he offered them, let them go somewhere else."[50] But Diering did use the detailed surveys available after 1876; Edgar was reacting to what may have been a high-handedness

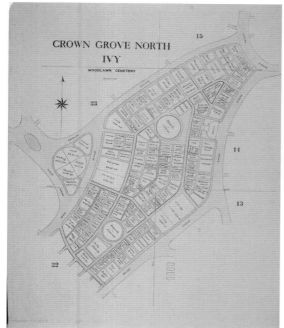

Fig. 31. Plan of Beech plot with Havemeyer circle at its center and Crown Grove plot (southern section) showing early multiple paths defining circular and elliptical lots. Avery Library, Drawings & Archives, Woodlawn Cemetery Records.

Fig. 32. Crown Grove plot from above with circular R.H. Macy lot in the middle. Photograph by Gavin Ashworth.

he projected at the end of his long tenure. Diering's control of Woodlawn's design emerged during the early days of the circles. Those of Farragut, Marshall O. Roberts, the Havemeyers, and others, were influenced by Whiting and probably Batterson, but their later proliferation as a characteristic landscape form was due to Henry J. Diering.

By 1875 Crown Grove plot was mentioned in the annual report: "it will be justly esteemed one of the most attractive plots yet opened: to meet a demand for lots separated from each other with gravel paths, the Trustees determined to lay out this plot with isolated circular, oval, and square plots." (Figs. 31, 32) By 1878 there were ambitious plans for even bigger circles: "The Trustees have decided to make the entire Central Avenue front of [Evergreen] Plot in three large pieces, the corner of Central and Poplar Avenues being a circle of one hundred feet in diameter, and the other two being very large square pieces surrounded on three sides by wide gravel paths ... a feature in cemetery design not undertaken heretofore." Cornelius Vanderbilt Jr. bought the circle and Joseph Pulitzer bought one of the large squares. By 1882, Woodlawn had created its largest circle lot in Lakeview plot – so large that it is surrounded by a road rather than a path. It was sold to Jay Gould for $60,000. Its size was singular, but there were other circles tangent to it – all of them floating in a continuous field of gravel paving. Against the gravel, the dome shaped circular lawns stood out almost like separate planets. It was here that the "circles of sepulcher" defined Woodlawn's most characteristic landscape feature.[51] (Figs. 33, 34)

The growing use of paved paths to separate lots coincided with new rules made in 1876 forbidding fences, hedges, or enclosures on new lots. In the interest of keeping a smooth continuous ground plane, the cemetery began asking permission to remove hedges from lot perimeters and

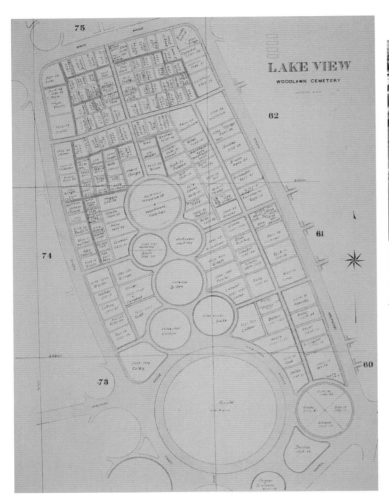

Fig. 34. Large circles in Hawthorn and Lakeview Plots. William Hall obelisk foreground, with Jay Gould mausoleum in the left distance. Gould's is the largest circular lot at Woodlawn. Photograph by Gavin Ashworth.

Fig. 33. Lakeview plot with large, adjacent circles of varied sizes was laid out along the high ground of the cemetery in the 1880s. Avery Library, Drawings & Archives, Woodlawn Cemetery Records.

then in 1878, doing so without charge. Woodlawn bought twenty-five lawn mowers in 1884 and began cutting the grass for free in 1886. As historian David C. Sloane has observed, cemetery managers preferred to control such maintenance so they could control the appearance of the cemetery.[52] New lots that were isolated by paved paths sold at a premium and they were also much easier to mow and maintain than old ones with fences or hedges (Fig. 35).

The success of Lakeview plot was followed in the 1890s by similarly grand compositions of hill-top circles at Oak Hill and Walnut plots and by other large circles along Central Avenue. Some of these sites had ledge rock just below the surface making burials more difficult there, but the sites were ideally suited to above ground structures. The grand mausoleums and monuments that crowned these lots were commissioned from the era's greatest architects: McKim, Mead and White; Carrère and Hastings; Peabody and Stearns and even Henri Deglane, an atelier master at the École des Beaux-Arts.[53] Their size, artistic quality, and location on high points, reinforce the hierarchy suggested by topography. They define the monumental landscape style of Woodlawn. Diering's concentration on these plots was touted in the annual reports in the late 1890s: "We have laid out this year a large number of lots in circular form, of various sizes, more particularly designed for those desiring lots separate from the surrounding ones, thereby filling a demand which is constant and growing."[54]

As cemetery designer Jacob Weidenmann observed, "In the lawn system the boundary of a circular lot is difficult to retrace."[55] He was pointing out that "lawn plan" lot divisions were discreetly marked and made nearly invisible to suggest a communal, natural landscape. Scholars have shown how Olmsted, Strauch, and others in America were influenced by Prince Hermann von Pückler's writing and his landscape park at Muskau in Saxony and, perhaps less directly, by landscape descriptions in Goethe's novel, *Elective Affinities*, where the reform of a cemetery is specifically described: "Sparing, as far as possible, the old monuments, [Charlotte, the Baroness] had contrived to level it, and lay it carefully out, so as to make it appear a pleasant spot on which the eye and the imagination could equally repose with pleasure."[56] Romantic landscape ideas of German origin inspired the "lawn plans" of Strauch and Weidennmann, but Woodlawn's adoption of the plan's principles and its Romantic communal character was half-hearted. The cemetery lacked leaders committed to enforcing its tenets and, perhaps more crucially, high land values made Woodlawn's trustees reluctant to sacrifice saleable ground to provide the generous communal open space the "lawn plan" required.

Woodlawn's "circles of sepulcher" evolved into a style of cemetery landscape quite different from the picturesque and naturalistic ideals of the "rural" cemetery or the continuous, communal sweep of the "lawn plan." The circles integrate building (or monument) and landscape into a single monumental form. Each one is isolated by a paved perimeter that contains and defuses the radiating axes implied by its architecture. Though they resemble small City Beautiful components, the circles resist the axial or geometrical relationships so characteristic of that planning style. Rather, these architecture/landscape forms are separated and juxtaposed, one circle with another. The matrix of interconnected circles holds these landscape monuments tightly together and a formal order is imposed upon, or at least draped over, the shaped undulating topography like a net. The eclectic individuality of privately landscaped lots sometimes strains against this order, but as cemetery maintenance has declined, individuality has been eroded and the shared landscape structure has prevailed.

Fig. 35. Woodlawn began using lawn mowers in the 1880s. This photograph illustrates the fleet of mowers in the mid-twentieth century. Avery Library, Drawings & Archives, Woodlawn Cemetery Records.

The Perimeter

After the early years, the trustees concentrated on financial and real estate issues and this led to acquisition of land to expand the cemetery. In May, 1874 Woodlawn bought 3.5 acres from William Booth and James Smith along with 56.75 acres from Hugh Camp; in June, 1875, half an acre was acquired from James Valentine; and in March, 1879, 26 acres from J. Hugh Peters, Absalom's son. According to John Jay Smith, the cemetery paid $1,250.00 per acre for this additional land. At about the same time, a few more acres were purchased for stables across 233rd Street from the north service entrance. All these parcels enlarged the cemetery from its original 307.5 acres to 396.3 acres.

By 1887, the cemetery had sold just eighty-seven acres for burials, less than a quarter of its land, but the $2,324,045.52 sale price of these lots yielded payments to The Associates of $1,162,022.76. In the twenty-three years of operation, they had made nearly ten times their initial investment. Though the land purchases of the 1870s nearly doubled The Associates' original investment, three quarters of Woodlawn's land was still available for future sale.[57] This additional land enlarged the cemetery to the southeast, but a problem arose there in 1883 when the city condemned a strip of land and constructed a water main that awkwardly divided the parcel. Had the terrain been flat and even, the pipe could have been run underground, but it crossed a deep ravine and a stone aqueduct was needed to carry the water line. This impeded development there until the 1930s when the waterline was abandoned and the city sold the land back to the cemetery.

The city surrounding Woodlawn was in constant flux and changes at the cemetery's perimeter profoundly affected its development. In 1874, southwestern Westchester County, where Woodlawn was located, was annexed by New York City as the 23rd and 24th wards. This led to a street planning scheme by Frederick Law Olmsted Sr., whose report recommended against construction of a road running along the west side of the railroad (though his plan suggested one between Woodlawn and the railroad).[58] If this plan had been adopted, it would have made smoother connections between the cemetery and its surroundings, so its rejection had negative consequences for Woodlawn. The road between the railroad and the cemetery continued to be discussed until the city acted in 1897 to take a long strip of property for construction of Webster Avenue. This cut deeply into Wood-lawn's steep hillside and required a tall retaining wall along its eastern property line – changes that disrupted the visual connection of the cemetery to the Bronx River Valley. Construction forced the cemetery to close the northern section of its Central Avenue near Chapel Hill plot for several years to adjust its grade and width. The City's $157,354.16 award for taking this land might have helped defray the cost of the wall, but some of The Associates sued for half this sum, which they would have been entitled to if the land had been sold as cemetery lots. In 1902 the court ruled in their favor and Woodlawn was forced to pay out half the award plus the court costs. Before Webster Avenue was complete, changes to 233rd Street began. This included another retaining wall to accommodate its rolling topography to the newly level road and a new bridge over the railroad and the Bronx River. For nearly five years traffic at the main entrance to the cemetery was disrupted. The long-term consequence was a landscape whose rolling topography is jarringly disconnected from its surroundings by retaining walls.

The situation along Jerome Avenue was more complicated, but eventually it resulted in a better outcome for the cemetery. The City proposed a scheme to extend the Grand Concourse to Jerome Avenue and beyond to the new northern city line. This would have required condemnation of cemetery property and also James Valentine's adjacent parcel at the corner of Jerome and 233rd Street. Another city right of way, then called Mount Vernon Avenue, further complicated the situation. It extended the line of what is now Van Cortlandt Park East from 233rd Street to Jerome Avenue. The cemetery was able to prevent the taking of its land, and eventually this section of Mount Vernon Avenue was de-mapped in 1905. Several years of negotiations with Valentine followed and in 1907 Woodlawn completed its last expansion with the purchase of his land for $100,000 (Figs. 36, 37).

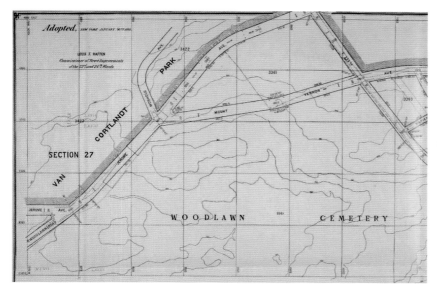

Fig. 36. Mount Vernon Avenue between 233rd Street and Jerome Avenue in an 1898 New York City map (west is up). This unbuilt street separated a triangle of Woodlawn's land from the rest of the cemetery. It was "demapped" in 1905 reconnecting the two parts of the cemetery and Woodlawn then acquired the parallelogram parcel (shown with a dashed line) in 1907. Avery Library, Drawings & Archives, Woodlawn Cemetery Records.

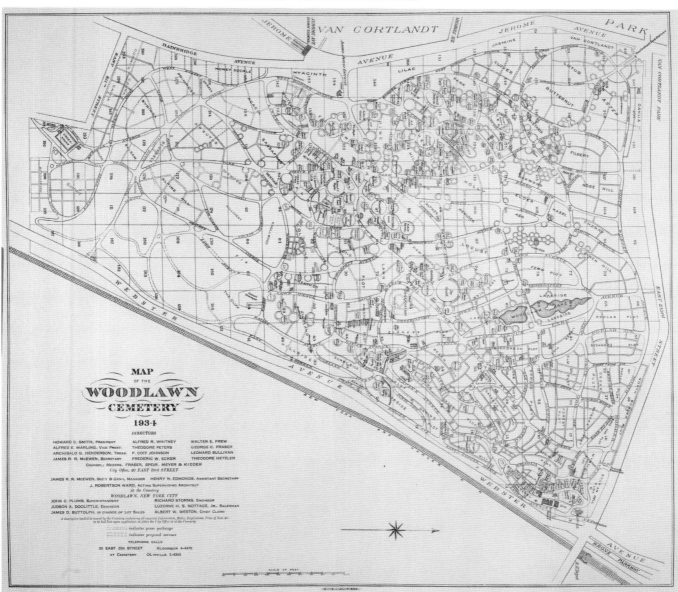

Fig. 37. Woodlawn expanded its perimeter until 1907; this view from 1934, shows the extent of development before World War II. In 2013 there is still undeveloped land within its boundaries. Avery Library, Drawings & Archives, Woodlawn Cemetery Records.

Charles H. Edgar and Reform

The nineteenth century concluded unhappily at Woodlawn. In 1895, William A. Booth, who had led the cemetery's trustees since its inception, died and was replaced by James D. Smith. This was soon followed by the departure of Caleb B. Knevals as Vice President and Comptroller and his replacement by Charles H. Edgar in August 1899. At the end of 1900, Henry J. Diering, the landscape gardener and Superintendent who had nurtured the cemetery landscape from the beginning, retired and was succeeded by his son, Frederick R. Diering.

Knevals departure was quickly followed by his disgrace, his death, and the discovery that his estate was bankrupt. Circumstances revealed that he had fraudulently issued Woodlawn Associates scrip (stock certificates) and used it as collateral on a personal loan from American Exchange National Bank in 1893. After repaying the loan, he took out another one in late 1900. When Knevals failed to make payments on the 1900 loan, the bank discovered the fraud and Woodlawn then learned of it, too. The bank could not recover money from Kneval's bankrupt estate, so it sued Woodlawn. Appeals dragged on until 1907 when Woodlawn was forced to pay the debt plus interest and court costs.[59]

Woodlawn was an intergenerational project and even the changes caused by this dramatic upheaval were gradual. In 1902, Charles H. Edgar, son of one founder and nephew of William Booth, wrote to a fellow trustee, Charles S. Smith, son of board president James D. Smith, describing the conditions he found in the cemetery and city office when he succeeded Knevals: "It seems to me that it would have been better for the cemetery, if three years ago we had cleaned house thoroughly and had Caleb B. Knevals and his nephew, [Woodlawn Assistant Treasurer] Charles F. Knevals, arrested. … A year ago, when I thought I had found everything, [the American Exchange National Bank suit] turned up; and after we had forgiven Caleb B. Knevals he worked in every way against us." Edgar asserted that the legal fees paid to Knevals's brother Sherman, the cemetery's counsel, were excessive and fumed at the large annual outlay to the three Knevals. Other trustees were accused of greed: "Certain directors seem to think that they should obtain all the money possible for their own object. They do not look forward for the best interests of the cemetery and lots-owners. We are put there as trustees for the lot-owners and we should manage our trust in the most conscientious way." He outlined the steps he had taken to reorganize the office and place the affairs of the cemetery on a solid footing as he condemned his colleagues for actively working to undermine his diligent efforts. Edgar wondered if his shaky executive control would last long enough to make Woodlawn a modern business operation. It was a pained assessment coming from an executive who claimed to hold "more scrip in my name individually or as a trustee than is controlled by any other member of the board."[60]

Edgar's critique extended to cemetery planning and Henry Diering's preoccupation with large lots: "There is [an] impression abroad, which, in my opinion, should be overcome, and that is that only the rich can buy lots at Woodlawn. … We should invite the small and medium lot-owners back." In April, 1904 Edgar sent another letter, this one to the whole board. It is far less plaintive in tone, but it reiterates the need for small lots and laments the drain on Woodlawn's finances caused by large payments to The Associates, $477,625.00 (four times the cost of the original land) in the four years 1900-1903. With Edgar, a cleansing reform began at Woodlawn.[61]

Edgar's push for smaller lots resulted in a new way of laying out plots. Frederick R. Diering devised smaller circular lots of nearly identical size and arranged them in tight groups. Sometimes the groups were in the middle of plots such as Birch Hill, Juniper, and Dogwood, and these resulted in similarly sized monuments held in a web of tangent circles to form dense compact ensembles distinct from the surrounding landscape. Another concentration of small circles along Woodlawn's northern Park Avenue resulted in rows of similarly scaled mausoleums, with equal setbacks from the avenue. They have an urban character akin to a Manhattan side street; it is a memorable departure from the nearby sections of more varied circles designed by his father. There had always been smaller individual monuments built on smaller lots, which were developed and sold among the large circles. They often comprise a beautiful landscape that derives its character from adjacency to large mausoleums and the open space that came along with them. The system of smaller circles instituted by Edgar and the younger Diering often substitutes greater uniformity of scale for the complex hierarchy of the earlier sections (Figs. 38, 39).

New, large lot circles were also designed under Frederick Diering, but it is notable that Golden Rod and Hickory plots, laid out between 1904-07 have irregular lots accommodating exposed ledge rock at their centers. These plots extended the scheme developed in the 1880s and 1890s across the high ground of the cemetery's southern center, but reveal a trend away from the imposition of geometry and toward a more naturalistic landscape. The Olmsted's design of the Constable lot of the same period is indicative of the same trend (see Fig. 81) (Fig. 40). The mix of lot shapes and sizes in the twentieth century plots developed under the younger Diering demonstrate his ability to extend the "circles of sepulcher" style established by his father while adapting it to changing tastes and different topography. By 1921 when Myostosis plot was

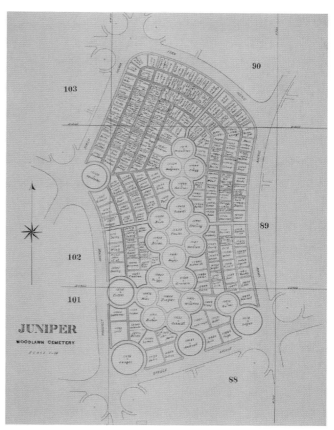

Fig. 38. Juniper plot, illustrating how small circles were grouped at the center of a plot, providing open space at the center of the plot and making it possible to sell less valuable internal land for more money. Avery Library, Drawings & Archives, Woodlawn Cemetery Records.

Fig. 39. Dogwood plot, from Fern Avenue to Elder Avenue. Though some of the circular paths are now overgrown, their dome-shaped landforms and complex rotated orientation are illustrated here. After 1900, groups of adjacent, similarly-sized circles were used to organize several plots. Photograph by Gavin Ashworth.

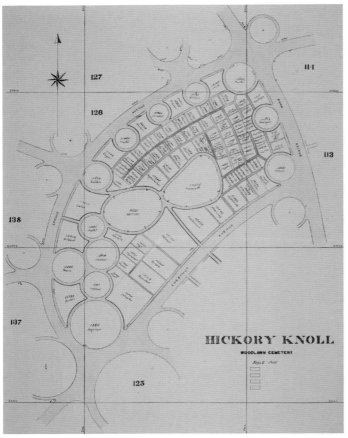

Fig. 40. Hickory Knoll plot. Irregular lots taking advantage of natural ledge rock and topography indicate a resurgent naturalism after World War I. Avery Library, Drawings & Archives, Woodlawn Cemetery Records.

laid out, the last of the big circles appeared on the plan. Woodlawn's dominant themes were set and its character established. It remained for designers of individual lots to build upon this legacy (Fig. 41).

After the Great War

Just as the Civil War had renewed interest and spurred change in memorial design, so too, did victory on the European continent in 1918. American battlefield cemeteries and monuments in Europe shared many features with the cemetery at Gettysburg. In both places burials were marked by simple repetitive stones radiating from a single monument or a chapel. The superb quality of these American cemetery landscapes and memorials in Europe synthesize the previous eighty years of American cemetery design and reflect the influence of Woodlawn. Many World War I monuments and buildings in the European cemeteries were designed by architects and sculptors who worked at Woodlawn. These include John Russell Pope; Charles A. Platt; York and Sawyer; Paul Manship; Egerton Swartwout (unbuilt at Woodlawn); and the British architect, Sir Edwin Lutyens. Many share Woodlawn's close integration of architecture, landscape design, and decorative arts including sculpture and stained glass. Centralized control by the American Battle Monuments Commission led to unity of design. It was not so different from the way Woodlawn's engineer Judson Doolittle and Superintendent Frederick

Fig. 41. John C. Plumb carving a clay model of mounded circles circa 1940. Designs for new plots that followed the pre-World War II pattern of large circles were revised to accommodate smaller repetitive lots after the war. Avery Library, Drawings & Archives, Woodlawn Cemetery Records.

R. Diering worked with the architects and landscape designers on private mausoleums. In both places the topography was groomed to create lawn settings that fused architecture and decorative arts to form a memorial landscape that was itself monumental.

This close integration of art, architecture, and landscape was what Woodlawn's designers aspired to from its founding. Landscape styles had continuously changed along with the style of the plastic arts, but the European victory brought confidence and prosperity in its wake, and this allowed American architects to refine the eclecticism that is such a notable characteristic of Woodlawn's architecture. Landscape artists, too, had benefitted from decades of careful study, looking to European precedents and techniques to find ideas that were adaptable to American circumstances. The result of this at Woodlawn was a collaborative approach that enabled multiple artists working together on single projects to achieve a highpoint in the artistic development of the cemetery which lasted until 1929.

As Andrew Dolkart shows in the essay that follows this one, the shared landscape provided a framework for a diversity of architectural styles and the complexity of cultural reference entailed in such variety. Woodlawn is a verdant gallery for the display of treasured images collected from distant places, many of them framed by an encircling path. This is, after all, not only characteristic of Woodlawn, but also of the arboreal urban structure used widely by the Olmsteds and other American town planners. Its similarity to residential suburbs of the early twentieth century is striking. There, too, styles are freely mixed: Colonial Revival houses sit comfortably next to their Tudor, Norman, or English Georgian neighbors. Different cultural references are subsumed within similarities of function and scale. Lot separations in both cemetery and suburb are gently enforced by curved pavement and well-tended shrubbery in a smooth continuity of turf under a grand canopy of ancient trees. These designed landscapes are as remote from the jostling city as they are dependent upon it. The urbanism of life and death are somehow the same.

Fig. 42. Simple repetitive headstones in Fir plot. This became the standard design pattern after World War II. Photograph by Gavin Ashworth.

After the Great Depression and the Second World War, mausoleums on large individually landscaped plots became a vestige of the past – too costly to build and out of tune with the economic leveling that accompanied steeply progressive post-war taxes. The cemetery's plans for more large circular lots at the center of newly opened plots gave way when demand for small individual burial lots organized with simple monuments in even rows took hold (Fig. 42). These arrangements spread across the gentle slopes of the cemetery's south eastern sections with the same pleasant monotony that defined the mass-produced houses carpeting former farm fields around every American city. The community mausoleums constructed in this era, too, have an analog in the banal apartment blocks put up after the war.

Today Woodlawn's landscape is a composition of remarkable coherence and beauty. As Central Avenue ascends from the cemetery's entrance at Woodlawn Station along Sidney's steep and twisting route, it emerges on rolling ground where it follows more graceful curves. It is a timeline of cemetery design. This avenue passes great works of art and architecture sheltered among the ancient trees. It is unfinished as landscapes always are, but it is no longer as Absalom Peters found it:

> Awaiting here the hand of human skill, and taste,
> And toil, to smooth the roughnesses of nature's mould[62]

NOTES

1. Blanche M.G. Linden, Silent City on a Hill: Picturesque Landscapes of Memory and Boston's Mount Auburn Cemetery (Amherst: University of Massachusetts Press in association with Library of American Landscape History, 2007).

2. Drew Gilpin Faust, *This Republic of Suffering: Death and the American Civil War* (New York: Alfred A. Knopf, 2008).

3. James H. Moorhead, "The 'Restless Spirit of Radicalism': Old School Fears and the Schism of 1937," *Journal of Presbyterian History* 78:1 (Spring 2000): 29.

4. E.H. Gillett, *History of Presbyterian Church in the United States of America* (Philadelphia: Presbyterian Publication Committee, 1864), 2:513.

5. Edwin G. Burrows and Mike Wallace, *Gotham: A History of New York City to 1898* (New York: Oxford University Press, 1999) 268, 269, 452-454; Robert G. Albion. *The Rise of New York Port* (New York: Scribner, 1939), 250-251.

6. Bertram Wyatt-Brown, *Lewis Tappan and the Evangelical War Against Slavery* (Baton Rouge: Louisiana State University Press, 1997).

7. Vanderbilt's control of the both NY & Harlem Railroad and Hudson River Railroad gave him control of all rail lines into Manhattan. For an account of the Harlem corner, see T.J. Stiles. *The First Tycoon* (New York: Alfred A. Knopf, 2009), 376-380, 394-397.

8. Aaron V. Wunsch, "Emporium of Eternity." *Nineteenth Century* 28, no.2 (Fall, 2008):14-23.

9. John Jay Smith, *Recollections of John Jay Smith* (Philadelphia: J.B. Lippincott Co., 1892), 290.

10. Ibid, 291.

11. Hoadley and his first wife, Mary Hotchkiss, were uncle and aunt to Caleb B. Knevals's sister-in-law Mrs. Sherman Knevals. Her brother, Russell Hotchkiss was Woodlawn's assistant treasurer from 1868-81. Both families were from New Haven. Charles W. Knevals, the cemetery's Assistant Treasurer after Hotchkiss, was a nephew of Caleb B. Knevals.

12. Horace Clark was the son of Reverend Daniel A. Clark who succeeded Absalom Peters in the pulpit of his Bennington, Vermont, congregation; James Dickinson Smith's father was also a Presbyterian minister. Two of William Booth's sons were clergymen, and he built a church for the congregation of his home-town, Stratford, Connecticut. Though James A. Edgar was confirmed as an adult in the Episcopal Church, he was raised as a Presbyterian and his brother was Presbyterian divine.

13. Corporation records. Old Records Division, New York County Clerk's Office, New York. The Associates Land Co. was incorporated May 9, 1892, dissolved Dec. 15, 1924.

14. Henry E. Pierrepont, Green-Wood's founder, was also a founder of Grace Episcopal Church and David Bates Douglas, its planner, went on to lead Kenyon College, an Episcopal College in Ohio. Stephen Whitney attended Trinity Church.

15. Albion, *Rise of New York Port*, 250-251.

16. "City of the Dead," *New York Evening Mail*, July 31, 1870, clipping, Private collection of Merriman Gatch (hereafter cited as Gatch Collection).

17. *Annual Report of the Trustees of the Wood-Lawn Cemetery to the Lot-Owners for the Year* 1864. (New York: Office of the Wood-Lawn Cemetery, 1864). See Woodlawn Cemetery Records, 1863-1999, Drawings & Archives, Avery Architectural & Fine Arts Library, Columbia University (hereafter cited as Woodlawn Cemetery Records).

18. John W. Reps, *The Making of Urban America* (Princeton: Princeton University Press, 1965), 382-412.

19. Michael J. Lewis, "The First Design for Fairmont Park." *Pennsylvania Magazine of History and Biography* 130, no.3 (July 2006): 283-297.

20. I am indebted to Aaron Wunsch for supplying a list of J.C. Sidney's projects. Also see Aaron V. Wunsch, "Parceling the Picturesque: 'Rural' Cemeteries and Urban Context in Nineteenth-Century Philadelphia." (PhD diss., University of California, Berkeley, 2009).

21. Frederick C. Merry was born in England and immigrated to Camden, New Jersey, with his family. According to Merry's obituary, he too, worked on Fairmont Park. He was an early employee of George B. Post and eventually established a practice on his own. Merry worked with Sidney on Woodlawn's original buildings, but of those buildings, only the much altered stone cottage at the north entrance remains. He died March 4, 1900 and is buried at Woodlawn. See "Death List of the Day" *New York Times* March 6, 1900. For information on Merry's work with Post, see Balmori, Diana, "George B. Post: the Process of Design and the New American Architectural Office (1868-1913)" *Journal of the Society of Architectural Historians* 46 (Dec., 1987): 350.

22. William Avery Clift diary, Miscellaneous Personal Papers Collection, Record group 30, boxes 22-23, Yale Divinity School Library.

23. Ibid.

24. Frank Luther Mott, *History of American Magazines* (Cambridge, Mass.: Belknap Press, 1957-68), vol. 1-2. *The American Agriculturist* was edited by A.B. and R.L. Allen, whose agricultural activities in Erie County were well known. Absalom Peters likely knew them from his missionary activities in the area or through his brother-in-law, Samuel Wilkenson, who was mayor of Buffalo. By the time of Clift's involvement, the *American Agriculturist* had been taken over by Orange Judd, another Western New Yorker, interested in scientific agriculture.

25. The block between 26th and 27th Streets contained the separate depots of the NY & Harlem Railroad and the NY & New Haven Railroad, which ran on the same tracks from Madison Square to the fork just north of Woodlawn.

26. Minutes of the Woodlawn Executive Committee, Jan. 17, 1866, Woodlawn Cemetery Records.

27. David Hoadley to William A. Booth, Jan. 23, 1867, Gatch Collection.

28. R.E.K. Whiting report to David Hoadley, Dec. 1866. Gatch Collection. Whiting was born at Fort Hamilton in New York in 1833, the youngest son of an Army Colonel. He attended Bowdoin College for some time, and applied unsuccessfully to West Point in 1850 and 1851, apparently acquiring his knowledge of civil engineering from his brothers. In 1850 he helped survey a rail and canal route across the Mexican Isthmus of Tehuantepec. His eldest brother William H.C. Whiting, a brilliant, temperamental civil engineer, had graduated first in his class at West Point. He was put in charge of coastal defenses in San Francisco Bay in the 1850s at the same time David G. Farragut was establishing the Mare Island Naval Yard there. Robert followed him west where he joined a surveying party in Washington and Oregon in 1855 and another in the Sierra Nevada. Robert joined his other brother, Jasper, on a survey of Sonora in northern Mexico in 1858. They were expelled from Mexico by local authorities and camped for months in the remote, hostile Arizona desert waiting to be readmitted so they could complete their work. Robert became ill and returned to California and, eventually, to Hartford, Connecticut, where his widowed mother lived. When the Civil War broke out, both his brothers joined the Confederate Army (William H.C. Whiting as a Major General) and both died in the war, leaving Robert to look after his mother and sisters.

29. Whiting to Peters, June 25, 1867, Woodlawn Cemetery Records.

30. Minutes of the Woodlawn Executive Committee, Jan. 24, 1866, Woodlawn Cemetery Records.

31. Whiting report on Spring Grove Cemetery, Oct. 12, 1867, Woodlawn Cemetery Records.

32. Ibid.

33. Thomas Belknap, a founder of Cedar Hill Cemetery was Whiting's father-in-law. Just days before writing the Spring Grove Cemetery report, Whiting had asked for permission to marry Belknap's daughter Elsie, who was eventually related by marriage to James G. Batterson. See Whiting to Thomas Belknap, Oct. 4, 1867, and Wedding invitation, Gatch Collection.

34. James G. Batterson founded New England Granite Works in 1845. The company expanded quickly, acquiring quarries in Westerly, Rhode Island, and Concord, New Hampshire. It was noted for its Civil War monuments in Gettysburg and Antietam and for major building projects such as the Connecticut State Capitol and the Library of Congress. The company developed and benefitted from innovations in steam-powered machinery for cutting and polishing granite. In New York City Batterson was a partner in Batterson, See and Eisele, a large enterprise that imported and fabricated marble and mosaic tile. In addition to his work in the domestic stone industry Batterson traveled widely, studied the monuments of Egypt firsthand and acquired a notable collection of paintings. He was the founder of the Traveler's Insurance Company. See *The Commemorative Biographical Record of Hartford County, Connecticut* (Chicago: J.H. Beers & Co., 1901), 23-28.

35. Whiting report on Spring Grove Cemetery, Oct. 12 1867. Woodlawn Cemetery Records.

36. Nehemiah Cleaveland, *Green-Wood Illustrated* (New York: R. Martin, 1847).

37. R.E.K.Whiting to Elsie Whiting, Oct. 9, 1870, Gatch Collection.

38. Clinton Monument Association, *The Clinton Monument MDCCCXLVIII* (New York: Van Norden, 1848), 8-12.

39. Linden, *Silent City on a Hill*, 95-116.

40. Robert W. Habenstein and William M. Lamers, *The History of American Funeral Directing* (Milwaukee: Bulfin Printers, 1955), 323-351.

41. Charles Crary to R.E.K. Whiting, March 23, 1871, Gatch Collection.; R.E.K. Whiting report to William A. Booth, April 13, 1868, Woodlawn Cemetery Records.

42. R.E.K. Whiting to Elsie Whiting, Oct. 17, 1870, Gatch Collection.

43. R.E.K. Whiting to Elsie Whiting, Sept. 9, 1871, Gatch Collection.

44. Evidently Knevals's firm repeatedly bribed customs' inspectors. Once caught, the correspondence of his firm was splashed across newspaper pages, but the fines they paid were a small fraction of their gains. Undeterred, they were caught again in 1873; this time, shoes and fine silks were found intermingled with the sugar samples. (*Daily Graphic* (New York), May 25, 1874, 645, 648.) Knevals was Superintendent of the Sunday School Society at the Broadway Tabernacle Church and a director of the American Tract Society. It is notable that his brother Sherman was the law partner of Chester A. Arthur after 1872. Arthur was Collector of the Port of New York in charge of the Customs House from 1871-1878. Knevals had other investments including Sniffen Court in Manhattan, which he built in partnership with another Woodlawn trustee, James D. Smith.

45. Griswold Report, n.d., Woodlawn Cemetery records.

46. Woodlawn's city office had been the headquarters of the Committee of 70, an anti-Tweed reform group of which Havemeyer was vice-president.

47. John Claudius Loudon, *An Encyclopaedia of Gardening; Comprising the Theory and Practice of Horticulture, Floriculture, Arboriculture and Landscape-Gardening* (London: Longman, Hurst, Rees, Orme, Brown, and Green, 1824), 51.

48. William S. Pelletreau, *Historic Homes and Institutions and Genealogical and Family History of New York* (New York, Chicago: Lewis Pub. Co., 1907), 208-210.

49. Minutes of the Woodlawn Executive Committee, Sept. 11, 1872, Woodlawn Cemetery Records.

50. Charles H. Edgar to Charles Stewart Smith, Nov. 21, 1902, Woodlawn Cemetery Records.

51. *Annual Report … Wood-Lawn,* 1873 and 1878, Woodlawn Cemetery Records.

52. David Charles Sloane, *The Last Great Necessity* (Baltimore, Johns Hopkins University Press, 1991), 126, 238-39.

53. *Supreme Court of New York, Appellate Division – First Department. Austin W. Lord, et al. against Kenneth M. Mur-*

chison, Jr. with Washington Hull. Case on Appeal (New York: Payne Printing Co., 1902). Court testimony indicates that the front elevation of the William A. Clark Mausoleum was scaled down, but otherwise followed the design produced by Henri Deglane. And that the interiors and other elevations were designed by Lord, Hewlett & Hull, and K.M. Murchison, Jr., Associated Architects.

54. Woodlawn Cemetery Annual reports 1897-1899, Woodlawn Cemetery Records.

55. Jacob Weidenmann, *Modern Cemeteries* (Chicago: Monumental News, 1888), 21.

56. Elizabeth Barlow Rogers, "What is the Romantic Landscape?," in *Pückler in America ,* ed. Sonja Duempelmann, Bulletin of the German Historical Institute Supplement 4, (Washington, D.C.: German Historical Institute, 2007), 11-26.

57. Smith, *Recollections*, 290n. The 87 acres sold includes both the actual lots sold and the roads and paths surrounding them. For a summary of land transactions and cemetery finances, see *Documents of the Senate of the State of New York*, 110th session, 1887, Vol. 4, Doc. 68.

58. Charles Capen McLaughlin, ed., *The Papers of Frederick Law Olmsted*, vol. 7, *Parks, Politics and Patronage, 1874-1882* (Baltimore: Johns Hopkins University Press, 1977-1992), 343-344.

59. *Report of Cases Heard and Determined in the Supreme Court of the State of New York,* Vol CXX (Albany: J.B. Lyon Co, 1907), 119-133.

60. Edgar to Charles Stewart Smith (undated), Woodlawn Cemetery Records.

61. Edgar to Charles Stewart Smith (undated), Minutes of the Woodlawn Executive Committee, Woodlawn Cemetery Records.

62. Peters, Absalom, "City of the Silent" *Hours at Home* 3 (May-October, 1866): 79-82.

DESIGNING WOODLAWN:
BUILDINGS AND LANDSCAPES

ANDREW SCOTT DOLKART

In his memorial to Frederick R. Diering, the long-time superintendent of Woodlawn Cemetery, early twentieth-century cemetery critic Ernest Stevens Leland proclaimed that "world-renowned architects, landscape architects and sculptors together with noted memorialists, able horticulturalists and the large staff of able experts retained by the cemetery organization have made this cemetery a mecca for lovers of art and nature, a shrine of the commemorative arts and an archetype of the ideal modern cemetery."[1] Leland's description captures what makes Woodlawn Cemetery such a compelling concentration of architectural and landscape design: the collaboration of many of America's finest architects and landscape architects, in concert with "memorialists," i.e., firms that specialized in designing mausoleums and other cemetery monuments, and other artists and professionals. This essay will trace the history of that collaboration, focusing in particular on the early decades of the twentieth century when the number of burials in the cemetery rose significantly and when designers prominently contributed to the creation of the cemetery's character.

In the rural cemeteries founded in America between the 1830s and 1860s, including Woodlawn, established in 1863, the cemetery corporation was responsible for creating an environment that would attract people to purchase lots. Thus, from the very start, design was key to establishing the character of the cemetery. Woodlawn's founders hired English-born engineer James C. Sidney to transform the farm fields and wood lots into a carefully-planned rural landscape.[2] Although Sidney was only active at Woodlawn until 1867, his plans for grading the land, delineating lots, landscaping the site, and creating an undulating system of major and minor roads and paths, and several water features became a template for the early development of the cemetery as a picturesque landscape.

While the general design and maintenance of a cemetery was the responsibility of the cemetery corporation, the design of individual lots was usually left to their owners, subject to certain restrictions. Thus, owners could erect simple markers commemorating the death of an individual or they could erect large and costly mausoleums, set into a hillside or freestanding. They were also allowed to surround their lots with iron fences, hedges, or other adornments. This approach is especially evident at Green-Wood in Brooklyn, the earliest rural cemetery in the New York City area, founded in 1838, where scores of impressive, sophisticated mausoleums, many in the Gothic, Classical, and Egyptian styles, were erected in the nineteenth century. The architects of most of these structures cannot be identified because cemetery corporations did not require drawings for these early mauso-

PLATE 2. Harbeck mausoleum in Parkview plot at night. Photograph by Gavin Ashworth.

DESIGNING WOODLAWN   53

Fig. 43. The Gothic Revival style Eccles Gillender mausoleum (circa 1880) in Ravine plot, by an unknown designer. Photograph by Gavin Ashworth.

leums and did not keep detailed records of what were essentially private construction projects, and also because few architectural archives survive from this period.[3] Far fewer mausoleums were erected at Woodlawn in the 1860s through the 1880s than at Green-Wood. Although Woodlawn was founded several decades after Green-Wood, it too did not maintain records of mausoleum designs and designers. The massive granite hillside facade of Addison Gould Jerome's family tomb (circa 1868) and the handsome Eccles Gillender mausoleum (circa 1880) (Fig. 43) resembling a small Gothic chapel, are two of many examples that were probably designed by architects now unknown.

For several decades after Woodlawn's founding, most wealthy New Yorkers continued to choose Green-Wood as their place of burial. But Woodlawn's founders appreciated that the city was rapidly growing northward and that southwestern Westchester County (which was annexed to New York City in 1874) would eventually be more desirable for burial than Brooklyn. An 1866 *New York Times* article comparing the advantages of various New York area cemeteries noted the convenience of Woodlawn, emphasizing that the founders designed the cemetery

> to have it more accessible than any of the other cemeteries in the suburbs. These, with
> the exception of Trinity [in northern Manhattan], all lie across navigable waters, and are
> approached by crowded streets and ferries. These occasion delays to the funeral processions,
> and often furnish sights and sounds very little in keeping with the wounded sensibilities
> of the sorrowing. In the approaches to Woodlawn, the public have the advantage of steam-
> cars and a railway. . . . Funeral parties with the remains of their dead are conveyed by
> special trains in thirty-five minutes from any of the City stations on the Harlem Railroad
> to the main entrance of the cemetery. By contract made with the railroad company,
> separate cars can be chartered for this purpose.[4]

By the 1890s, the prescience of Woodlawn's founders was confirmed as New Yorkers, increasingly living in neighborhoods north of 42nd Street, chose Woodlawn as their preferred place of final rest.

Woodlawn in the late nineteenth and early twentieth centuries offered burial sites that were far different from those planned by Sidney and the original founders of Woodlawn. By the late 1860s, the cemetery's administration had rejected the rural cemetery idea – with its intricate pattern of major and minor roads and paths, and lots adorned with fences and hedges – in favor of the "landscape lawn" plan, which offered broader, gently curving roads, large plots uninterrupted by paths that would be divided into lots, including many that were circular, and open lawns unobstructed by fences and hedges.[5] One commentator noted in 1896 that while "it was customary to enclose lots either with stone curbing, iron railings or natural hedges" thirty years ago, "Woodlawn is to-day conspicuous for the absence of such relics of bygone practice, the officials of the cemetery having persuaded the lot owners to allow of their removal, and now very few remain, giving great satisfaction."[6] Instead, carefully placed trees and the monuments and mausoleums became focal points within the unobstructed expansive greensward. Photographs from the late nineteenth and early twentieth centuries show the mausoleums and other monuments set on lawns, a series of photographs published in 1905 by monument manufacturer Robert Caterson illustrates the preponderance of the landscape lawn idea at Woodlawn, with almost every image showing the lawn extending right to the walls of a mausoleum.[7] Plantings on individual lots were limited to small shrubs or low formal flowerbeds such as those at the 1903 mausoleum of Hannah Elias (Fig. 44). In addition, many mausoleums incorporated stone urns overflowing with seasonal plantings.

Fig. 44. The Hannah Elias mausoleum in Juniper plot is set on a lawn ornamented with low, formal flower beds. *Monumental Work of Robert Caterson* (Bronx: Robert Caterson, 1905). Avery Library, Classics.

Mausoleums

People of varied income levels had been buried at Woodlawn since its founding, but beginning in the 1880s many of the wealthiest people in America chose Woodlawn for their burial. These wealthy families commissioned mausoleums and expansive monuments in numbers and on a scale that had not previously been seen in this country. *Park and Cemetery*, the leading journal of the cemetery industry, noted in 1899 that mausoleums were "generally few and far between" because of their cost, but that Woodlawn was the exception, having "the distinction of possessing, a large number of such memorials, the cost of which as a collection is proportionately far in excess of the outlay for such buildings in perhaps any cemetery in the world of its age."[8] The article is accompanied by images of five mausoleums that document the scale and flamboyance of the new monuments erected by newly wealthy American industrialists (Fig. 45). Railroad magnate Jay Gould erected a grand Ionic temple (1884, probably designed by H.Q. French, a specialist in the design of cemetery memorials), purported to be "the best specimen of pure Grecian architecture in the United States," in the center of the largest circular lot at Woodlawn; shipbuilder and philanthropist William H. Webb is memorialized in a dynamic Baroque structure capped by a conical roof (circa 1892); chemical and corset manufacturer Dr. Lucien C. Warner commissioned an elegant tholos supported by Corinthian columns and decorated with a Tiffany mosaic ceiling (1888); Henry Flagler, a founder of Standard Oil and later a railroad and hotel tycoon, built a round Romanesque style mausoleum for his deceased wife, with a domed top reminiscent of those on early churches in the Poitou region of

Fig. 45. Five of Woodlawn's most prominent early mausoleums were illustrated in *Park and Cemetery* in October 1899. *Park and Cemetery* 9 no.8 (October 1899), 173. Avery Library.

France (1881); and, grandest of them all, was railroad magnate Collis P. Huntington's enormous 1891 Classical temple by mausoleum designer and manufacturer Robert Caterson, set on a rise adjoining the entrance to the cemetery, with double flights of stairs leading to a terrace.[9] Huntington's project cost $250,000 and was reputed to be the most expensive mausoleum in the world.[10] Architects have been identified for only two of these buildings: R.H. Robertson for Warner's mausoleum and Thomas Hastings for the Flagler project.

Why Warner hired Robertson remains a mystery. Although Robertson was a prolific architect, there is no evidence of his ever working with Warner before receiving the commission for the family mausoleum. Warner's dynamic Queen Anne house in Harlem was designed by A.B. Jennings and his one known commercial commission went to William Tuthill; both architects were still active in 1888 when Warner commissioned his mausoleum.[11] In contrast, Hastings had a close relationship with Flagler. Flagler worshipped at the Presbyterian church where Hastings's father was the pastor and it must have been Reverend Hastings who introduced Flagler to his young son. This mausoleum was an early commission, dating from before Hastings established a partnership with John Carrère, and before the Carrère & Hastings firm had designed five important buildings for Flagler in Florida.[12]

The fact that some wealthy people had the same architects design their mausoleums and monuments that they had commissioned for their city houses, country houses, and other buildings is an important aspect of Woodlawn's design history. This patron-architect loyalty is especially evident in the six Woodlawn mausoleums designed by McKim, Mead & White, the most prestigious architectural firm in America at the turn of the twentieth century. All but one, the John W. Sterling mausoleum (1910), a beautiful Greek Doric temple in antis, were designed for families that had previously commissioned buildings from the firm. However, Sterling, a founder of the prestigious law firm of Shearman & Sterling, had close business and social connections with those who had commissioned buildings from McKim, Mead & White, most notably Wall Street financier Charles J. Osborn and his wife Miriam. Stanford White had designed Tahoma, the Osborn's picturesque country house overlooking the Long Island Sound in Mamaroneck, New York (1883-85), and in circa 1893, the firm designed the Osborn's enormous round marble mausoleum at Woodlawn (Fig. 46).[13]

Fig. 46. Osborn mausoleum in Brookside plot, designed by McKim, Mead & White, circa 1893. Neg. #892428. Collection of New-York Historical Society.

Other McKim, Mead & White clients also retained the firm to design their Woodlawn mausoleums. Henry E. Russell, a founder of Russell & Erwin, a New Britain, Connecticut, hardware manufacturer, had commissioned one of McKim, Mead & White's earliest masterpieces, the 1883-85 RusWin Hotel in New Britain, Connecticut. Following his death in 1892, his wife Elizabeth Russell commissioned the firm to design the family's monumental Roman Classical mausoleum. The famous caterer and restaurateur Louis Sherry, who had commissioned the Narraganset Casino in Rhode Island and several New York City restaurant buildings from McKim, Mead & White, chose the firm in 1905 as the architect for his small, but elegant, domed mausoleum, which would remain vacant until his death in 1925. Robert and Ogden Goelet, real estate developers and financiers, had commissioned houses and commercial buildings from the firm, and in 1898 commissioned a monumental mausoleum with a design based on the tomb of Mausolus (from which the word "mausoleum" comes) at Halicarnassus. National City Bank director Henry A.C. Taylor, whose Newport mansion and New York City townhouse were both designed by McKim, Mead & White, hired the firm to design a tall domed structure in the form of a Greek cross with elaborate sculptural ornament in honor of his wife Charlotte, who died in 1899 (Fig. 47). Not only were these McKim, Mead & White tombs impressive designs, located on large and prominent sites and built of the finest stone, but they were also finished with exquisite details – mosaic ceilings, carved sarcophagi, Guastavino vaulting, and windows by Tiffany Studios – echoing the quality of craft in the firm's houses and other large-scale works.

Many other leading American architects were also commissioned to work at Woodlawn in the

Fig. 47. Henry A.C. Taylor mausoleum in Walnut plot, designed by McKim, Mead & White in 1899. Avery Library, Drawings & Archives, Woodlawn Cemetery Records.

early twentieth century, including Henry Colt Albro; William Welles Bosworth; John Duncan, Heins & La Farge; William Mead Howells; Hunt & Hunt; Peabody and Stearns; Charles A. Platt; John Russell Pope; Renwick, Aspinwall & Tucker; James Gamble Rogers; Trowbridge & Livingston; and Warren & Wetmore – sometimes working for former clients and sometimes designing for new ones. Some families hired lesser known or totally obscure architects, in some instances because of past experience with their designs. For example, Edward Necarsulmer, a little known architect with an eclectic career, who designed Franklin Simon's Fifth Avenue department store, created an austerely simple octagonal mausoleum for the Simon family in 1926, eight years before Simon's death (Fig. 48).

Problems often arose, however, with the quality of mausoleums designed by architects who did not have experience designing this unique type of building. Mausoleums are deceptively simple buildings. Although small in scale with a single interior space and no need for utilities, such as gas, electricity, or water, they are extremely complex buildings with a unique set of design problems and constraints. The successful mausoleum would, of course, be a beautiful structure. William Henry Deacy, a leading proponent of artistic monument design, noted that "anything built to last forever should be above all things beautiful and so … [this] must dominate the builder's creed."[14] The basic

Fig. 48. Franklin Simon mausoleum in Butternut plot, designed by Edward Necarsulmer. Photograph by Gavin Ashworth.

requirement of a building planned to last forever was the choice of durable materials. This explains why mausoleums are built of stone, with those from the late nineteenth and twentieth centuries generally constructed of durable granite or, to a lesser extent, marble or limestone. Durability also explains why the doors and window frames are almost always bronze. Beyond the choice of materials, many other issues and details were necessarily the focus of designers who specialized in mausoleums. For example, sealed joints to prevent water penetration were of paramount concern. Mausoleum architect Ferdinand Procházka was unequivocal in his belief that "the first principle to follow is to avoid upright joints in the projecting mouldings and roof of the mausoleum."[15] Since doors and windows would rarely be opened, ventilation was also crucial and quite complex, requiring designs that would assure that interiors were dry and that condensation would be kept to a minimum.[16] Among the most complex challenges was the construction of the mausoleum roof to assure that there would be no leaks. Roofs with either a large single stone or large slabs laid in a stepped manner, with no vertical joints, were used where possible, insuring, as one monument catalogue assured, "the permanent and water-tight construction so indispensable in mausoleums."[17]

While some architects, such as McKim, Mead & White, met the challenges of mausoleum design, others did not have this specialized knowledge. Although a specialist in mausoleum design with a self-interest in attracting clients to his own firm, Procházka was correct when he warned that an architect could have a "preconceived notion of style and form" that was inappropriate for a mausoleum and find it hard "to separate himself from a form which, as far as construction goes, is likely to become a failure."[18] Because of this need for such specialized knowledge and experience, architects actually received relatively few mausoleum commissions and some of those who did were ignorant of what was needed for a successful project. In 1912, for example, Richard Storms, Woodlawn's chief engineer, wrote to John Downey, the contractor erecting the mausoleum for railroad tycoon and philanthropist Joseph Milbank designed by the prestigious architectural firm of York & Sawyer (best known for its banks), calling attention "to the roof which in time is sure to leak and cause trouble." Storms recommended that "a roof of entirely different design should be substituted."[19] Similarly, in 1919, Storms responded to the design prepared by architect James Layng Mills for Mary L. Schoonmaker's mausoleum, warning of problems with the plan, including the grade of the ground and the thickness of the foundation walls, and, echoing Procházka's comment, noting that "eight exposed vertical joints in the roof and an equal number in the cornice which are sure to leak and cause serious trouble unless raised joints with bronze caps are provided."[20]

Memorialists

The vast majority of mausoleums and monuments at Woodlawn and other American cemeteries were designed by monument companies, or memorialists, that specialized in this type of construction. These companies proliferated in the late nineteenth century as the demand for cemetery monuments increased. Some were local, catering to clients at a specific cemetery, but others became well-known national firms designing and manufacturing hundreds of monuments and mausoleums each year, some custom designed and others constructed from stock plans. Many of these companies had their offices adjoining cemetery entrances, where the bereaved could purchase a mausoleum after buying a lot. A 1909 business directory lists five monument firms at Woodlawn.[21] Among the firms located close to Woodlawn's main entrance were those of Robert Caterson and Lazzari & Barton (Fig. 49), both of which designed and/or constructed many important early structures at the cemetery. Caterson, for example, was responsible for Collis P. Huntington's mausoleum (see Fig. 45) and Lazzari & Barton for the impressive, domed John F. Martin mausoleum (Fig. 50). Other firms had their offices and showrooms in Manhattan on major streets such as Fifth Avenue and Broadway, where they could conveniently serve both those looking for a memorial for a recently deceased relative and those seeking to build one for their own future use.

While some monument firms produced awkward, ill-proportioned work, many were anything but second-rate artisans. Several firms had talented architects on their staffs. Indeed, many of the

Fig. 49. Workers posing at the Lazzari & Barton stoneworks, located across from the entrance to Woodlawn Cemetery. Lazzari & Barton. *Mausoleums* (New York: Lazzari & Barton, 1903). Avery Library, Classics.

Fig. 50. Lazzari & Barton created the John F. Martin mausoleum in Pine plot in 1909. Avery Library, Drawings & Archives, Woodlawn Cemetery Records.

largest, most beautiful, and most expensive mausoleums and other monuments at Woodlawn were commissioned from these firms. Farrington, Gould & Hoagland exemplifies the quality of work produced by these companies. The firm was founded in the early twentieth century and was first known as Stone, Gould & Farrington. In about 1913, Franklin R. Farrington, John R. Gould (a graduate of Columbia's architecture school), and George S. Hoagland created the Farrington, Gould & Hoagland company, with its offices and showroom on Broadway. By 1927, when they published a marketing catalogue, the company had designed at least eighty-six mausoleums and over one hundred other monuments at Woodlawn.[22] The catalogue details the scope of the firm's abilities:

Our service as Memorial Designers and Builders embodies under one contract the entire work from preliminary consultations, sketches and plans to the delivery of the finished Memorial; centralizing responsibility and expediting completion. Our staff of Memorial Architects have had years of experience and exceptional training, and we specialize exclusively in the art, architecture, and scientific construction of Memorial Monuments, Mausoleums, and Statuary… Our work ranges in size from a Headstone to the largest Monument or Mausoleum.[23]

Fig. 51. Charles and Delloria Gates mausoleum in Pine plot, designed and constructed by Farrington, Gould & Hoagland, 1912. *Farrington Gould and Hoagland, Incorporated : memorial designers and builders : mausoleums, monuments, statuary* (New York : Farrington Gould & Hoagland, Inc., 1927). Avery Library, Classics.

The text ends with the boast: "Our Clients are our References." While this is, of course, marketing hyperbole, the scale of many of Farrington, Gould & Hoagland's memorials and the prestige of their clients supports the truth of this claim. Some of the largest and most distinguished mausoleums at Woodlawn were designed and built by them, many from enormous slabs of Barre, Vermont granite, such as the 1912 Classical temple of Charles and Delloria Gates (Fig. 51), which *Park and Cemetery* recorded in 1915 as the most expensive mausoleum in the country and which *American Landscape Architect* noted in 1932 was "perhaps the most impressive [mausoleum] in Woodlawn," and the 1919 enormous Egyptian repository of the remains of five-and-dime magnate Frank W. Woolworth (see Figs. 85, 86).[24]

Another firm of memorialists, Presbrey-Leland, created the largest number of twentieth-century monuments and mausoleums at Woodlawn. This firm (later renamed the Presbrey-Leland Studios) was established in 1920 with the merger of two major New York firms – the Presbrey-Coykendall Company (itself the result of an earlier merger between the C.H. Presbrey and Louis Coykendall) and the W.W. Leland Studios.[25] The merger combined Presbrey-Coykendall's plant in Barre, Vermont (soon moved to Brattleboro, Vermont), where white granite from its own quarry at West Dummerston, Vermont or from other quarries was carved into monuments with their smaller plant adjoining Kensico Cemetery in Westchester and Leland's floral establishment on the corner opposite the main entrance to Woodlawn, which was converted into an office, showroom, and factory for memorials. One critic noted that this merger "combined one of the best known retail manufacturing concerns [Presbrey-Coykendall] with one of the best known firms specializing in design."[26]

Most of Presbrey-Leland's memorials were both designed and manufactured by the firm, which considered memorial art to be "a specialized branch of architectural design."[27] The design aspects of the new firm were in the hands of Columbia-trained architect William Henry Deacy, who had previously led the design department at the Leland firm and had given it the "reputation for high class work."[28] Deacy worked with a team of other trained professional architects and draftsmen.[29] The new firm marketed the talents of its design staff, claiming in one of its early catalogues that "the Director of Design and his Staff, in charge of the Studios, are registered architects of exceptional academic training and experience who are specialists in the design of Memorials and Mau-

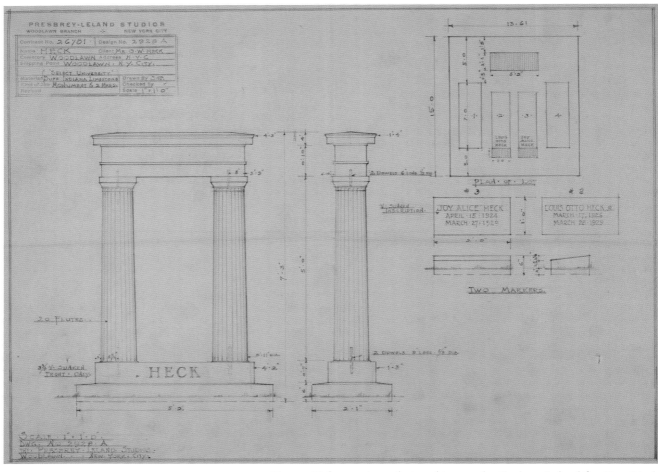

Fig. 52. Column screen designed in 1930 by Presbrey-Leland for Otto Heck mausoleum in Primrose Plot. Avery Library, Drawings & Archives, Presbrey-Leland collection.

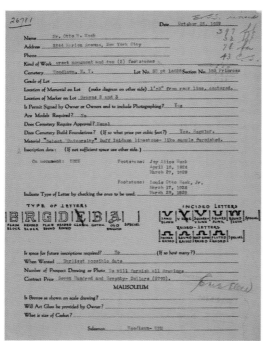

Fig. 53. Presbrey-Leland's order form permitted a client to choose the type and style of lettering for a monument. Avery Library, Drawings & Archives, Presbrey-Leland collection.

soleums."[30] The design team prepared extensive drawings for every project, with elevations, plans and details. For example, front and side elevations and a plan appear on the drawing prepared for the Doric column screen commissioned by Otto Heck in 1930 (Fig. 52). As is evident on the Heck drawings, the firm paid special attention to the design of inscriptions. The order form prepared for each project has graphic representations of various letter types (block, rounded, Gothic, Old English, etc.) and also asks if the letters should be incised or raised and in what style (Fig. 53). Full-scale drawings were then prepared for these inscriptions. For other projects, the design team also prepared detailed ornamental drawings. For the curved bench commissioned by Lillian Edwards as a memorial to her husband, songwriter Gus Edwards (whose most famous song was "Schooldays"), Presbrey-Leland not only pre-

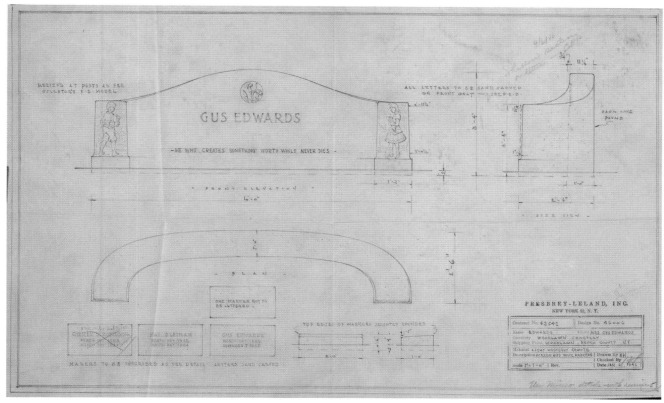

Fig. 54. Presbrey-Leland's design of a bench for composer Gus Edwards includes relief panels of a school boy and girl by sculptor Charles Keck. Avery Library, Drawings & Archives, Presbrey-Leland collection.

pared elevations and plans, but also details of a floral roundel and sketches of a pair of relief panels of a school boy and girl designed by sculptor Charles Keck (Fig. 54).[31]

The firm also took commissions for the manufacture of mausoleums and monuments designed by private architects. Its advertisements bragged that "the foremost American architects are constant patrons of the Presbrey-Leland organization. They appreciate meticulous workmanship."[32] At Woodlawn, the firm worked with Walker & Gillette on several projects, including the austere mausoleum for the family of banker Ernest Stauffen (1920) (Fig. 55); with Carrère & Hastings on the elegant domed, Neo-Classical mausoleum of Julius Stein (1916); and with McKim, Mead & White for John W. Sterling's grand mausoleum (1910) and the simple stone cross and headstones for Hermann Schwab (1934).

Presbrey-Leland maintained a public showroom, first at 11 East 47th Street and then on Fifth Avenue. For many years the firm occupied two floors at 681 Fifth Avenue between East 53rd and 54th Streets, where drawings, photographs, and scale models of monuments and mausoleums were on display (Fig. 56). The company advertised exten-

Fig. 55. Ernest Stauffen's mausoleum in Golden Rod plot, was designed in 1920 by Walker & Gillette and manufactured by Presbrey-Leland. Avery Library, Drawings & Archives, Presbrey-Leland collection.

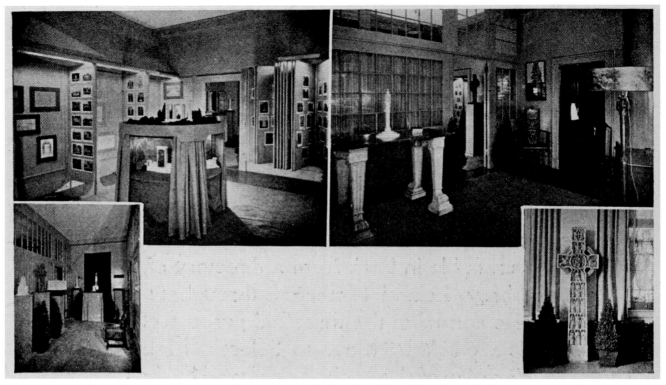

Fig. 56. Presbrey-Leland's showroom at 681 Fifth Avenue. *Book of Presbrey-Leland* (New York: Presbrey-Leland, 1929). Avery Library, Classics.

sively in newspapers, with images ranging from small headstones to enormous mausoleums, always providing the address of their showroom and inviting those interested to request one of the firm's illustrated catalogues. They also placed many full-page ads in the professional journal *Park and Cemetery*, suggesting that "cemetery authorities ... may recommend a visit to the gallery of memorial art."[33] Smaller branch showrooms were located in Hartford, Nashville, and Atlanta; salesmen traveled throughout the country marketing Presbrey-Leland's work. At the main New York showroom, potential clients could examine the variety of the company's memorials, discuss ideas with the design staff, and place an order. But, if a client needed a finished memorial immediately, they were available at the branch office at Woodlawn.[34]

Mausoleums are the most visible of the monuments at Woodlawn. Indeed, Woodlawn has more mausoleums than any other cemetery in America. They vary widely in scale and design, but all, no matter how relatively modest, bespeak the client's affluence. As *Park and Cemetery* commented, "the mausoleum is distinctly the monument of the well-to-do, for whether we take the small and unpretentious structures, worthy of the name, it is a question of degree of wealth only."[35] At Woodlawn, the siting of a mausoleum was crucial, since its location within the landscape is often as much a signifier of prestige as its design. The most expensive lots tend also to be those that are most prominently visible from major avenues. Many of grandest mausoleums are located along and near Central Avenue, which extends through the cemetery from the original main entrance near the Woodlawn railroad station in gently undulating curves to the Jerome Avenue entrance adjoining the subway. The cemetery sections closest to Jerome Avenue & Pine, Fairview, Oak Hill, Walnut, and Myosotis – were opened for development in the late nineteenth and early twentieth centuries. These sections were divided into large lots purchased by New York's elite. As a result, Central Avenue as it runs between these plots is especially rich in architecturally distinguished mausoleums. Other nearby sections, along Park Avenue to the south of Central Avenue and in the Golden Rod, Parkview and Chestnut Hill sections to the north, include large lots with distinguished monuments set in more secluded locations. Many of the grandest mausoleums are on the circular lots that are a defining feature of Woodlawn's plan, with the large central circle owned by an especially wealthy family and smaller circular lots arrayed around it. Other important mausoleums are located on corner sites or on irregularly shaped lots at the juncture of avenues (see Fig 1). It is clear that even in death, many wealthy people were intent on conspicuous display. Mausoleum owners who were less wealthy and could not afford the prime lots, often acquired sites set back from the road, where their memorial might be partially blocked from view by other monuments, or smaller lots on streets, such as Park Avenue north of Central Avenue, or on narrow paved paths that were densely lined with similar structures, in effect creating neighborhoods of upper-middle-class mausoleums (Fig. 57).

Fig. 57. Park Avenue lined with modestly-scaled mausoleums set close together on small lots. Photograph by Gavin Ashworth.

Mausoleum Styles

The vast majority of the mausoleums at Woodlawn, as at other American cemeteries, are Classical in design, ranging from a small Greek temple with pilasters or a pair of columns to monumental structures with peripteral colonnades and flights of stairs, such as William Ziegler's circa 1899 (Fig. 58). But Classically-inspired designs came in many variants. Some lot owners chose an antique style modeled after the octagonal Tower of the Winds in Athens, such as the William Charles Stewart mausoleum designed by John Russell Pope in 1914 (Fig. 59), or commissioned circular monuments resembling a Greek tholos or Roman temple (Trowbridge & Livingston's Vermont marble Doric temple for J. P. Morgan partner William H. Porter, designed in 1927, is among the grandest). Oth-

Fig. 58. William Ziegler's peripteral temple in Aster plot, designed circa 1899. *Monograph on the Work of the Tayntor-Davis Granite Corp.* (New York: Tayntor-Davis Granite, 1927). Avery Library, Classics.

Fig. 59. William Charles Stewart mausoleum in Heather plot, designed by John Russell Pope in 1914, after the Tower of the Winds in Athens. Photograph by Gavin Ashworth.

ers preferred Egyptian-inspired monuments of various scales, such as the elaborate version of Trajan's Kiosk at Philae, built for financier Julius Bache, designed by Davis, McGrath & Kiessling in 1915 and manufactured by Farrington, Gould & Hoagland (see Fig. 89); or F. W. Woolworth's which is enormous in scale (Farrington, Gould & Hoagland, 1919) (see Figs. 85, 86); or more modest ones which took the form of a Classical temple embellished with a cove cornice, lotus columns, winged disks, and other ancient Egyptian features.

Still others modeled their mausoleums on Baroque sources. Presbrey-Leland's 1924 mausoleum for bank note printer George H. Kendall and his wife Harriet resembles, in miniature, a seventeenth-century Italian church (Fig. 60). Still others were modeled after Gothic chapels. The most prominent

of these is architect Hunt & Hunt's adaptation of the late fifteenth-century French Gothic Chapel of St. Hubert at Amboise in the Loire Valley, commissioned by Alva Belmont for her husband Oliver Hazard Perry Belmont, immediately after his death in 1908 (Fig. 61). More typical are mausoleums resembling medieval English chapels, such as that designed by J. Robertson Ward and manufactured by the Harrison Granite Company for James D. Hurd in 1929, a stone structure of rock-faced random ashlar with a pointed-arch entrance and a connected wing wall with built in bench (Fig. 62).

In the late 1920s and the 1930s, austere, rectilinear mausoleums, with entrances set in stepped or curved recesses and often with stepped roof slabs, were designed in a Moderne style, or, as Presbrey-Leland referred to them, "Modernistic."[36] The large limestone mausoleum designed in the early 1930s by William H. Deacy for banker Phillip Lehman and his family is a striking example (Fig. 63). Presbrey-Leland described it as "an eloquent example of the monumental dignity to be attained by sheer simplicity of detail together with monolithic construction," noting that the

Fig. 60. George H. Kendall's Italian Baroque mausoleum, located in Butternut plot, by Presbrey-Leland, 1924. Photograph by Gavin Ashworth.

Fig. 61. Hunt & Hunt adapted the Chapel of St. Hubert at Amboise for the Belmont mausoleum in Whitewood plot, circa 1908. Chicago Albumen Works, Inc. (MNY240682), Museum of the City of New York.

Fig. 62. J. Robertson Ward's 1929 mausoleum for James D. Hurd, in Whitewood plot, was inspired by medieval English Gothic chapels. Avery Library, Drawings & Archives, Woodlawn Cemetery Records.

Fig. 63. The "Modernistic" Lehman mausoleum in Walnut plot, by Presbrey-Leland's chief designer William H. Deacy, early 1930s. Avery Library, Drawings & Archives, Presbrey-Leland collection.

Fig. 64. Ely Jacques Kahn's 1930 William R. Rose mausoleum in Columbine plot. Avery Library, Drawings & Archives, Presbrey-Leland collection.

vertical bands of the step-backed entry were "a modern note."[37] Another important example of a Modernist memorial is architect Ely Jacques Kahn's only known mausoleum, an austere, stepped mass designed in 1930 for lawyer William R. Rose, a founder of the Proskauer, Rose law firm (Fig.64).[38] Although a sharp-eyed viewer can find identical mausoleums built for different clients, since the monument companies had stock designs that they would use multiple times, a surprising amount of stylistic variety predominates at Woodlawn.

Monuments

Mausoleums were not the only choice of burial structures at Woodlawn, even for the very wealthy. The cemetery includes a wide array of monuments marking the sites where ground burial was chosen or where the deceased are placed in above ground sarcophagi. Some of these are elaborate monuments rivaling the mausoleums in their impressive design. The family of importer and art collector Hugo Reisinger, for example, erected an enormous polygonal colonnade on one of the most prominent sites along Central Avenue, done by Farrington, Gould & Hoagland in 1914 (Fig. 65). Nearby, the towering antique altar commemorating Hamilton McKown Twombly, a major figure in the running of the New York Central Railroad, and his wife, Florence Vanderbilt Twombly dominates a large circle (Fig. 66). The Twombly monument was designed in 1896 by McKim, Mead & White, who had also designed the family's estate in Florham Park, New Jersey, and was fabricated by the Ecclesiastical Department at Tiffany Studios. The monument for the family of textile manufacturer Matthew C.D. Borden, among the most spectacular at Woodlawn, designed by Carrère & Hastings,

Fig. 65. Farrington, Gould & Hoagland's polygonal colonnade in Oak Hill plot, for Hugo Reisinger, 1914. Avery Library, Drawings & Archives, Woodlawn Cemetery Records.

Fig. 67. William Henry McAlister monument in Highland plot, 1920. Avery Library, Drawings & Archives, Presbrey-Leland collection.

Fig. 66. Twombly monument in Oak Hill plot, modeled on an antique altar, by McKim, Mead & White, 1896. Avery Library, Drawings & Archives, Woodlawn Cemetery Records.

also occupies a large circular lot, centering on a marble sarcophagus modeled after that of ancient Roman consul Lucius Cornelius Scipio Barbatus preserved in the Vatican Museum (see Fig. 80). Borden's enormous sarcophagus is surrounded by smaller sarcophagi for other family members, all set on a podium with benches, balustrades, and urns. The design, shown at the annual exhibition of the Architectural League of New York in 1908, was extolled by the critic for *American Architect* as "a most satisfying and enduring work."[39]

Since the large monuments and mausoleums commissioned by wealthy families are the most visible design elements at Woodlawn, they are the almost exclusive focus of most accounts of the cemetery. However, they are only a small percentage of the structures at Woodlawn. Some of the most beautiful memorials are the smaller and highly varied exedras, balustrades, antique altars, benches, column screens, tablets, crosses, and other structures found throughout the cemetery. A few of these were architect designed, but most were the products of the memorial companies. Classical and Renaissance forms dominate. Most are set on lawns, often with ledger stones, foot stones, or head stones in near the monument. There is infinite variety in these architectural memorials – a bench with curved arms, interrupted in the center by a stone slab resembling an altar on which a name is written (William Henry McAlister, 1920) (Fig. 67); a balustrade interrupted by an altar crowned by an urn (David Theodore Davis, 1924) (Fig. 68); a sarcophagus set in the center of a lot surrounded by a balustrade with corner posts ornamented with swags and capped by urns (Alfred C. Chapin, designed by F. Burrall Hoffman Jr., 1909) (Fig. 69); a simple column screen (Heck Family, 1929) (see Fig. 52); a column canopy flanked by benches (Edward Zimmer, 1914) (Fig. 70); a long solid bench (Albrecht Pagenstecher, 1906) (Fig. 71); and a granite slab with a bronze portrait bust (Virginia Willeke, 1931, bust by Henry Hudson Kitson) (Fig. 72) are just a few of the variants found at the cemetery.

Fig. 68. David Theodore Davis monument, 1924 in Golden Rod plot. Avery Library, Drawings & Archives, Presbrey-Leland collection.

Fig. 69. Alfred C. Chapin's monument in Wintergreen plot, designed in 1909 by F. Burrall Hoffman Jr. Chicago Albumen Works, Inc. (MNY244989), Museum of the City of New York.

Fig. 70. Edward Zimmer monument in Golden Rod plot, 1914. *Monograph on the Work of the Tayntor-Davis Granite Corp.* (New York: Tayntor-Davis Granite, 1927). Avery Library, Classics.

Fig. 71. Albrecht Pagenstecher monument in Hickory Knoll plot, 1906. Avery Library, Drawings & Archives, Presbrey-Leland collection.

Fig. 72. Virginia Willeke monument in Golden Rod plot, with bust by Henry Hudson Kitson, 1931. Photograph by Gavin Ashworth.

Individual Landscapes

Many of the sites for the memorials were landscaped to frame the view towards the monument while screening out adjoining lots. The plantings generally consisted of evergreens of varying height to the rear and sometimes to the side of the monument. In some cases, flowers or ground cover were planted alongside the monument or adjoining ledger stones. The monument erected in 1936 by the Harrison Granite Company for Charles J. and Virginia T. Hardy along Lawn Avenue typifies this approach. The Hardys purchased a rectangular lot with a mature tree marking one of the corners. A rectangular stone with a gently curved top was placed near the rear of the lot; on the face of the stone is a horizontal band of foliage and the name HARDY in raised, somewhat rustic letters. Curved benches with the inscription, "He Giveth His Beloved Sleep," from Psalm 127 in the King James Bible, extend from either side of the stone tablet. In front of this ensemble, set within the lawn, is a large ledger stone embellished with a Celtic cross and a quote from the Song of Solomon, "Until the Day Break and the Shadows Flee Away." Herbert E. Smith, a landscape engineer from Patchogue, Long Island, was commissioned to landscape the lot. Smith's plan called for small clusters of shrubs (English yew, dwarf cypress, and lily-of-the valley) to either side at the entrance to the lot (Fig. 73). He surrounded the ledger stone with vinca, an evergreen ground cover, and clustered most of the planting to the sides and rear of the monument. Large rhododendron species and a single dogwood were placed at the rear edge of the lot, while smaller rhododendrons, yews, dwarf cypress, and other plants were set to either side. The landscape design created a backdrop for the monument, screening out the lots beyond, as is evident in the sketch that Smith provided with his plan.

Similarly, in 1917, Hans J. Koehler planned the lot for dry goods merchant Samuel Dwight Brewster. At the time of this commission, Koehler was a landscape architect in Wyomissing, Pennsylvania, but he had also worked for many years for Frederick Law Olmsted and Olmsted Brothers (including several projects at Woodlawn) and would eventually return to the Olmsted Brothers firm. The Brewster monument is a modest pink Tennessee marble sarcophagus, designed by architect Howard Major and carved by Presbrey-Coykendall, with modest ledger stones placed on the lawn marking the grave of each member of the family. The monument was placed towards the rear of the almost square lot, close to a walk that separates the lot from those of several larger mausoleums. Koehler created a dense planting of dogwoods, cedars, rhododendron, yews, and other plants that successfully screened out the surrounding memorials (Fig. 74).

Woodlawn also has a significant number of monuments placed on the round lots that are an important feature of the cemetery. On many of these round lots, approximately three-quarters of the circumference was densely landscaped, creating a single entrance and a strong frontal view of the monument. This approach was evident at the John and Helen Fahnestock Hubbard lot at the junction of Whitewood and Myosotis Avenues. In 1940 architect Phillip Hardie designed a cross set on octagonal steps and a pair of benches, which landscape architect Annette Hoyt Flanders surrounded with a carefully sculpted landscape of tall trees and lower shrubs, arranged in a formal geometric pattern to the rear and in more naturalistic groves to either side, none of which survive (Fig. 75).[40] The effect of an almost fully enclosed circle can still be partially experienced at Walter Graeme and Kate Macy Ladd's lot. Here, in 1934, architect Eric Kebbon designed a large curved bench set on a platform, with elegant carved detail. In front of the bench are two concrete crypts with ledger stones. To the sides were shrubs, while to the rear was a dense planting of evergreens, some of which are extant (Fig. 76). Other monuments were specifically designed to take advantage of an unusual landscape feature. In 1939 Therese Kuhn Straus purchased a lot with a large boulder to build a memorial to her parents Edward and Millie Kuhn. She commissioned architect James Gamble Rogers, who had previously designed the Woodlawn mausoleum for her in-laws, Isidor and Ida Straus (the owners of Macy's who went down on the Titanic), and landscape architect Ellen Biddle Shipman. Rogers and Shipman designed a

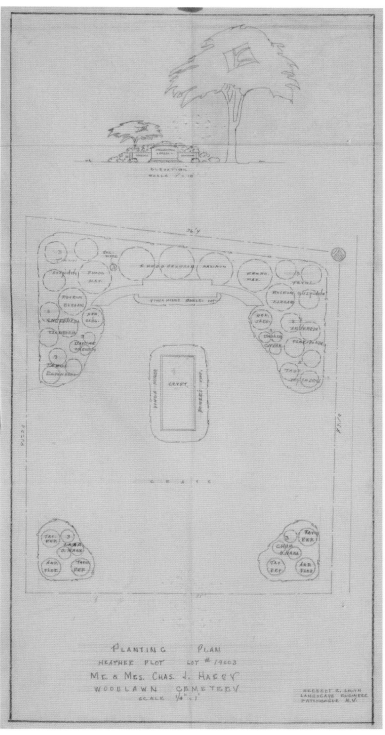

Fig. 73. Herbert E. Smith's planting plan for the Charles J. And Virginia T. Hardy lot in Heather plot, 1936. Avery Library, Drawings & Archives, Woodlawn Cemetery Records.

Fig. 74. Hans J. Koehler's dense planting scheme for the Brewster monument in Whitewood plot, 1917. Avery Library, Drawings & Archives, Woodlawn Cemetery Records.

Fig. 75. Phillip Hardie's cross in Walnut plot, designed in 1940 for John and Helen Fahnestock Hubbard, is set off by the landscape scheme of Annette Hoyt Flanders. Gottscho-Schleisner Collection, Library of Congress (#LC-G612-41240).

"burial garden" that would, as Rogers noted, "carry out the spirit of the huge boulder now on the lot," with the memorial and landscape "appear[ing] as though growing out of the big rock."[41] To achieve that effect, he created an alcove in front of the rock centered on a memorial tablet flanked by low, splayed ashlar walls with benches looking out onto a birdbath and stone walks, all set within Shipman's dense plantation of trees, shrubs, ground cover, and spring bulbs, including many plants set amidst the rocks (Figs. 77, 78, 79).[42]

This early twentieth-century proliferation of designed landscapes transformed the character of Woodlawn's landscape, challenging the precepts of landscape lawn design, creating a new type of cemetery landscape. Instead of the nineteenth-century emphasis on an open lawn interrupted only by monuments, roads, and the trees planted by the cemetery, the landscape of Woodlawn, especially in the sections to the west that were laid out in the early twentieth century, was now defined by a series of monuments on lots of varied size and shape, set within dense plantings that interrupted the flow of the lawns. Thus, Woodlawn became a mix of open landscape lawn plots and densely landscaped individual parcels, both large and small (see Fig. 1). Cemetery writer and critic Ernest Stevens Leland, the son of Presbrey-Leland partner W.W. Leland, an advocate for landscaping cemetery lots, observed that a mausoleum "invariably and inevitably requires a saving touch of Nature to relieve the inherent austerity of stone and to effect a pleasing transition from the abrupt verticality of the walls to the expanse of lawn."[43]

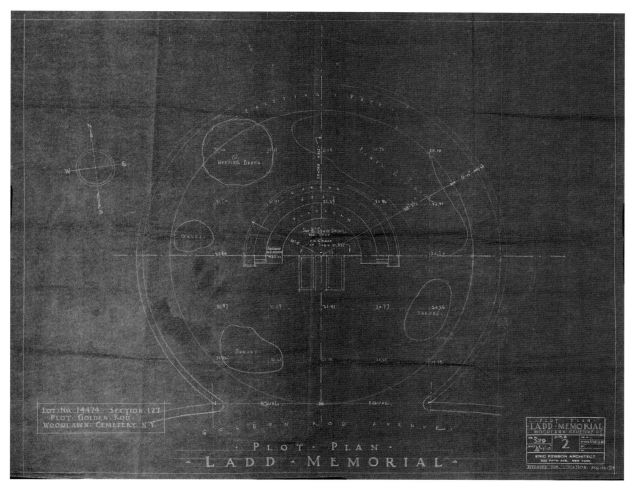

Fig. 76. Eric Kebbon's 1934 plan for Walter Graeme and Kate Macy Ladd's circular lot in Golden Rod plot. Avery Library, Drawings & Archives, Woodlawn Cemetery Records.

Fig. 77. Plan of the "burial garden," Knollwood plot, commissioned by Therese Kuhn Straus for her parents, Edward and Millie Kuhn; designed in 1939-1940 by James Gamble Rogers and Ellen Biddle Shipman. Avery Library, Drawings & Archives, Woodlawn Cemetery Records.

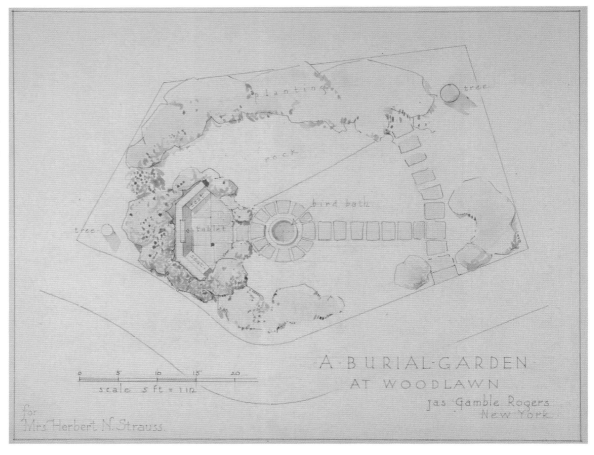

Fig. 78. Monument and bird bath designed by James Gamble Rogers for the Edward and Millie Kuhn lot in Knollwood plot, 1939. Avery Library, Drawings & Archives, Woodlawn Cemetery Records.

This new approach to the landscaping of individual lots coincided with the appointment in 1900 of Frederick R. Diering as Woodlawn's superintendent. Diering, the son of the previous superintendent, introduced new lot shapes and patterns. As Charles Warren has noted in this volume, Diering created large circles as well as clusters of small circles, laid out new sections with irregularly shaped lots, and planned lots of many different sizes.[44] It is not clear if the idea of individually landscaped lots was Diering's or, as seems more likely, was at least partially the result of the cemetery's wealthy lot owners demanding autonomy in designing their lots, especially in framing their monuments and screening nearby sites from view. Diering, however, officially approved each of the individual landscape designs whether they were those of highly skilled professionals or amateur gardeners. Leland, a vocal critic of what he called landscape lawn "extremists" who would sweep away all individual lot landscaping, argued for well-considered individual lot plantings.[45] He was a strong supporter of Diering and his policy at Woodlawn. "Mr. Diering's policy of an understanding, unbigoted, albeit critical supervision has at once encouraged creative effort the while persistently effecting an organized unity and harmony of massing throughout the vast grounds." Leland was especially impressed with how Diering was able to work suc-

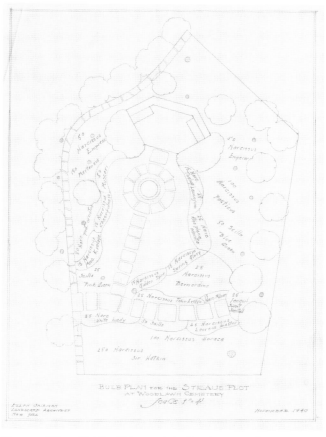

Fig. 79. Ellen Biddle Shipman's bulb planting plan, commissioned by Therese Kuhn Straus for the Edward and Millie Kuhn lot in Knollwood plot, 1940. Ellen McGowan Biddle Shipman papers, #1259. Division of Rare and Manuscript Collections, Cornell University Library.

cessfully with "the theorist and the practical gardener; the amateur and the specialist; the dilettante and the Fellow of the American Institute of Landscape Architects."[46] And while many of the private landscapes were undoubtedly the work of amateurs and, in many cases, probably the lot owners themselves, some of America's finest early twentieth-century landscape architects and designers completed miniature landscapes at Woodlawn. Landscapes have been identified by Adams & Manning; Sheffield A. Arnold; A.F. Brinckerhoff; Brinley & Holbrook; Marian C. Coffin; Beatrix Farrand; Annette Hoyt Flanders; Alfred Geiffert Jr.; James L. Greenleaf; Ruth Harvey; Mary Rutherford Jay; Hans J. Koehler; Charles Downing Lay; Charles Wellford Leavitt; J.J. Levinson; Olmsted Brothers; Prentice Sanger; Ellen Biddle Shipman; and Ferruccio Vitale, as well as many lesser known landscape architects, gardening companies, and florists. By the 1910s, Woodlawn's own staff was also preparing planting plans for individual sites at the behest of lot owners.

Individual landscaped lots had first appeared at Woodlawn in about 1904. Carrère & Hastings pioneered in this type of design with their monument for Matthew C.D. Borden (Fig. 80). Not only did the architect design the circle of sarcophagi for the Borden family, but they planned an arc of pleached trees to the rear of the ensemble clearly delineating the extent of the lot and focusing attention on the central aspect of the monument, Borden's own sarcophagus. The architects' in-

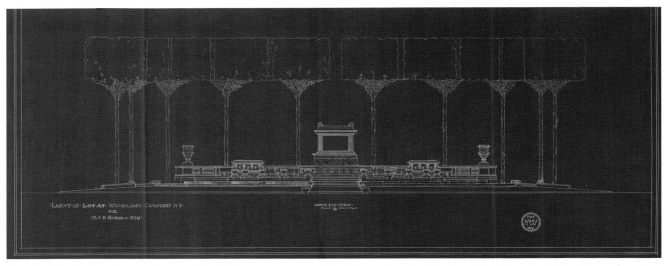

Fig. 80. Carrère & Hastings designed both the monument and landscape plan for Matthew C.D. Borden, in Fairview plot, circa 1904. Avery Library, Drawings & Archives, Woodlawn Cemetery Records.

tent is clearly evident on a beautiful Jugendstil-inspired elevation drawing that illustrates a series of slender trees with carefully shaped crowns hovering above and echoing the form of the monument (ultimately, conifers were planted instead, perhaps because of the expense of maintaining pleached trees).[47] Also dating from 1904 is the Olmsted Brothers design for the lot of yachtsman Cass Canfield, perhaps the first private commission at Woodlawn from a leading professional landscape architecture firm. Olmsted Brothers was the successor firm to that of Frederick Law Olmsted (designer of Central Park and Prospect Park), formed by Olmsted's stepson John Charles Olmsted and son Frederick Law Olmsted Jr. The Canfield commission was a minor project, consisting merely of a single tree and some vinca.[48] However, the next year, Olmsted Brothers received the commission for the Constable family lot, one of the most significant landscape projects ever undertaken at Woodlawn.

Louise Constable purchased an irregularly-shaped, rocky site along Park Avenue in 1904, following the unexpected death of her husband, Frederick A. Constable, head of the Arnold Constable & Co. department store. In 1905, at the suggestion of William Parsons, another prominent landscape architect who was brought in for a brief consultation, Louise Constable expanded the size of the lot. Although the Olmsted Brothers landscape would be the key feature of the lot's total design, the focus of the lot was a Celtic cross rising from the rocks, designed by William Schickel, the architect who had designed several large additions to the Arnold Constable department store which occupied much of the block between East 18th and 19th Streets, Broadway, and Fifth Avenue. According to Frederick Law Olmsted Jr., the site was chosen "because of fine group of old chestnut trees and rocky knoll. Mrs. Constable wants to keep it as retired and as quietly sylvan as possible. She likes the present appearance, but recognizes that the poison ivy and coarse weeds among the rocks and forming a ground cover on much of the lot, must be removed and something else substituted. I advised a strong background plantation behind the knoll, which was exactly in accord with her ideas."[49]

Besides the mature chestnuts, the site, as expanded under Parsons's direction, also included a mature tulip tree and a group of birches. As the design work progressed, the Olmsted firm, often represented by landscape architect Hans J. Koehler, and Constable settled on a design with two plantations of large evergreens (cedars, hemlocks, pines, rhododendrons, etc.) on the north and south sides of the lot, and herbaceous perennials, ferns, and dwarf evergreens on the rocks.⁵⁰ Early photographs show a rich array of colors and textures on the densely-planted rocky knoll, the cross rising from the rocks, and the taller evergreens screening out adjoining monuments (Fig. 81). A lawn adjoining Park Avenue contains Frederick Constable's headstone (and eventually those of other family members). The Olmsted firm continued to supervise maintenance of the Constable lot, trimming and augmenting the plantings and replacing dying plants, including substituting three red oaks for the chestnuts that succumbed to a blight

Fig. 81. Olmsted Brothers designed the complex landscape setting off William Schickel's cross on the Constable lot, 1904-1905. Avery Library, Drawings & Archives, Woodlawn Cemetery Records.

in 1907. The maintenance of this landscape was expensive and, in 1912, the clerk to Frederick Constable's estate asked Olmsted Brothers if costs could be reduced. The firm responded that "the lot has always been kept in excellent condition, and in dry summer weather, when other lots looked parched and sear, Mrs. Constable's lot has looked fresh and green. So, with one thing and another, we felt that if we made too many objections [to Woodlawn's administration] the lot might be allowed to deteriorate from that standard of excellence in appearance which Mrs. Constable seems to wish."⁵¹ After designing improvements to the planting in the spring of 1928, the Olmsted firm appears to have ceded general maintenance of the site to a local designer, James Tough, and correspondence between the firm and Mrs. Constable ceased.

The Constable lot is part of a major concentration of planned landscapes in the Walnut and Wintergreen plots, flanking Park Avenue, which were laid out and placed on sale in the early twentieth century. Together they once formed a virtually continuous landscape, with each lot's individual features interacting with those planted on neighboring sites. These lots display the various forms that designed landscapes adopted at Woodlawn during the early decades of the twentieth century as well as the pitfalls of creating landscapes that needed constant maintenance. Some were the work of leading American landscape architects, often working with prominent architects, while others were planned by nurseries. Several lots on or just off of Park Avenue echo the design of the Constable lot – a designed landscape planned around a relatively modest monument. This is evident on the lot acquired in 1909 by architect George B. Post for his family adjoining the Constable lot. Post, one of the most talented architects of the day, apparently designed the cross that is set towards the rear of the lot at the top of a slope and commissioned a landscape design from Marian C. Coffin. This was an early project for Coffin, who would become one of the leaders among the first generation of women professional landscape architects. Coffin planned a lawn that would sweep up the sloped lot to the cross, with planting beds marked by undulating edges along the side and rear of the lot, screening out neighboring monuments and framing the central cross.[52]

Nearby is the adaptation of the ninth-century Cross of St. Patrick and Columba (also known as the Saint Columbkille Cross) in Kells, Ireland, by Tiffany Studios for lawyer Charles D. Stickney and his wife Helen Hamersley Stickney. The cross was completely surrounded by specimen box-woods, fir, spruce, and cedar trees, juniper shrubs, and seventy-five rhododendron bushes, arranged by the Yonkers Nursery in 1912.[53] In 1918, for a lot nearby, McKim, Mead & White designed ledger stones and a strikingly original Greek cross set on a column. This monument was commissioned by Percy Pyne who previously had has McKim, Mead & White design his Park Avenue townhouse. James L. Greenleaf, a specialist in country house gardens, including that at Pyne's estate (Upton Pynes) in Bernardsville, New Jersey, created a landscape backdrop that screened the relatively small lot from lots to the rear.[54]

Several impressive mausoleums located on either side of Park Avenue demonstrate how the relationship between mausoleum and site had changed by the early twentieth century from the landscape lawn ideal of a building set on open turf to a new vision of a building set off by a planned

landscape that determined how it would be viewed and approached. Immediately across from the Constable lot is the rectilinear mausoleum of financier James Henry Lancashire and his wife Sarah designed in 1919 by the William D. Hawe Company, a New York City monument firm that received only a few commissions at Woodlawn. Although the mausoleum was quite simple, it originally sat within a complex landscape planned in 1922 by Mary Rutherford Jay, who referred to herself as a "garden architect" (Fig. 82). The mausoleum is placed towards the rear of a ninety-foot deep lot with a lawn in front opening onto Park Avenue. Jay preserved several mature trees on the lot and then designed irregularly shaped planting beds filled with azaleas and spirea shrubs set to either side of the entry to the lot.

Fig. 82. Mary Rutherford Jay's planting plan for the Lancashire lot in Wintergreen plot, 1922. Avery Library, Drawings & Archives, Woodlawn Cemetery Records.

The mausoleum entrance was flanked by mugho pines, a dwarf pine native to mountainous areas of Europe that was especially popular at Woodlawn, with beds of rhododendron, ferns, and narcissus extending to either side. Behind these plantings Jay placed dogwoods and Douglas firs that would rise above the lower shrubs and provide a backdrop to the mausoleum. This dense planting provide a strongly frontal alignment to the mausoleum, with the side and rear elevations virtually invisible.

Just south of the Lancashire, Constable, and Pyne lots lies the large site owned by the brothers Samuel H. and Rush H. Kress who ran the popular chain of five-and-dime stores that bore their name. Samuel was also one of the great collectors of old master paintings, which he donated to the National Gallery of Art, Washington, D.C, and other American institutions; he also established the Samuel H. Kress Foundation, which supports the study and conservation of European art. In 1921, the brothers decided to build a family mausoleum, probably in response to the death of Rush Kress's wife in 1915 and his son in 1921. Presbrey-Leland created one of its grandest Classical mausoleums for the Kresses, a rectangular building with trios of Corinthian columns at each corner supporting a full cornice from which rises a stepped roof. The pure white marble interior is lit by three medieval style stained-glass windows (*Faith*, *Hope*, and *Charity* by the Carlo Girard Studios of Florence). In 1925, the Kress brothers asked architect Theodore E. Blake to design the planting for the site (Fig. 83). Blake created an expansive scheme with irregularly-shaped beds of shrubs and mature trees in front, to the side, and behind the mausoleum, visually incorporating tall trees on the adjoining sites to the north into the wooded character of the landscape (Fig. 84). Blake planted over one hundred rhododendrons, as well as dozens of yew, azalea, holly, and dogwood plants. The lot is bounded to the south by curved paths that delineate the edges of the neighboring circular lots. From one path, Blake created a stone-lined walk leading into a small rock garden in front of the mausoleum. For many years, Rush assigned the gardener from his estate in Ossining, New York, to visit the site once a week and

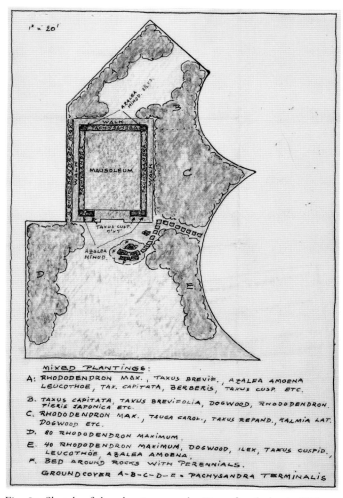

Fig. 83. Sketch of the plantings on the Kress family lot in Walnut plot. Avery Library, Drawings & Archives, Woodlawn Cemetery Records.

Fig. 84. Kress mausoleum in Walnut plot, designed by Presbrey-Leland in 1921, landscaped in 1925 by Theodore E. Blake. Avery Library, Drawings & Archives, Woodlawn Cemetery Records.

Fig. 85. F.W. Woolworth's mausoleum in Pine plot, designed by Farrington, Gould & Hoagland in 1919, before landscaping, with the George Ehret mausoleum to the left and the dome of the Armour mausoleum to the right. *Park and Cemetery* 32 no 2, April 1922, 39. Harvard University. Graduate School of Design. Frances Loeb Library.

Fig. 86. F.W. Woolworth's mausoleum in Pine plot, with Brinley & Holbrook's landscaping, with evergreens' screening the Ehret mausoleum to the left and the Harbeck mausoleum to the right. *Park and Cemetery* 32 no 2, April 1922, 39. Harvard University. Graduate School of Design. Frances Loeb Library.

care for the plantings. In 1939-40, the mausoleum was cleaned and extensive new plantings were incorporated, but at some point, perhaps after Rush's death in 1963, maintenance ceased and much of the magnificent landscaping that defined the building and its site has been lost.

Planned designs successfully melded the architecture and landscape at the Lancashire and Kress sites. Such unity was not easily accomplished. *Park and Cemetery* noted that the creation of landscape settings for mausoleums on large lots was a "landscape problem of no mean proportions." As the article also commented, the problem is "additionally complicated by the necessity of considering not only the lot itself but its relation to all of that portion of the cemetery in its immediate vicinity."[55] Thus, in many cases, it was not only necessary to consider how the plantings would relate to the individual mausoleum, but also how they would interact with the surrounding lots. Indeed, in many cases, the landscaping was specifically planned to screen out the surroundings, especially if a neighboring lot was home to an especially large monument. This was the case with Brinley & Holbrook's landscape for the F.W. Woolworth lot, which, at one-third of an acre, was among the largest in the cemetery. In the center of the lot stands Woolworth's large Egyptian mausoleum designed by Farrington, Gould & Hoagland. Before the landscaping was completed, the building was lost amidst a vista of competing neighboring buildings, including brewer George Ehret's enormous domed mausoleum designed by Schickel & Ditmars and manufactured by Robert Caterson (Fig. 85). The planting was planned to both emphasized the structure's scale and, at least partially, to screen out the neighboring mausoleums (Fig. 86). To that end, Brinley & Holbrook arranged the plantings in four irregularly-shaped beds filled entirely with evergreens, many of which were mature plants, some brought from as far away as Massachusetts and Virginia. "What a radical change the planting effected!," exclaimed Ernest Stevens Leland, "with almost magic facility the scene is transformed into a thing of beauty."[56]

While landscaping was generally used to enhance the view and setting of mausoleums and monuments at Woodlawn, the most interesting use of landscaping was as the memorial itself. At several sites the only architectural features are barely visible ledger stones set into the ground. At two examples along Park Avenue, these ledger stones were positioned within planned landscapes, one formal and architectonic, and the other, informal and naturalistic. The lot of architect Samuel Breck Parkman Trowbridge and his wife Sophia is a relatively small triangle on Park Avenue that appears to have been clipped off from a corner of the Lancashire lot. The lot's two ledger stones, each with a Celtic cross carved in 1925 by Harrison Granite Company and designed by the firm of Trowbridge & Livingston, were framed by English ivy and originally lay in the center of an octagonal "room" formed by yew hedges (Fig. 87).[57] Also within the octagon was a single bench by Trowbridge & Livingston. The corners outside of the octagon were filled with more informal plantings of azalea, mountain laurel, juniper, and a single flowering dogwood. This landscape was designed in 1925 by Ferruccio Vitale, a partner in the firm of Vitale & Geiffert. Vitale designed a number of country estates that frequently included enclosed gardens framed by clipped hedges, as he did on a much smaller scale for Trowbridge's memorial site. Unfortunately, by 1949, Woodlawn reported that the cost of caring for the hedge had increased and suggested that it be removed, which happened at an unknown later date.[58]

In contrast to the formality of the central portion of the Trowbridge lot, Beatrix Farrand, one of America's leading landscape architects, created an informal landscape for cotton and wool manu-

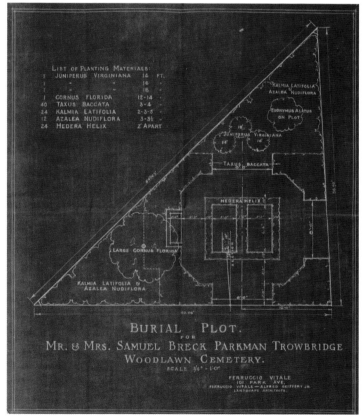

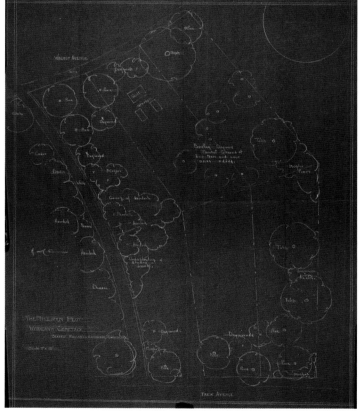

Fig. 87. Ferruccio Vitale's planting plan for the Trowbridge lot in Wintergreen plot, 1925. Avery Library, Drawings & Archives, Woodlawn Cemetery Records.

Fig. 88. Beatrix Farrand's informal landscape from the 1920s was the major feature of the Milliken family's plot. Avery Library, Drawings & Archives, Woodlawn Cemetery Records.

facturer Seth M. Milliken and his wife, probably in the 1920s shortly after Milliken's death. The lot fronts on Park Avenue and backs onto a quiet section of Walnut Avenue, with a narrow walkway separating it from the neighboring Constable lot to the north. Farrand scholar Diane Kostial McGuire notes that Farrand "believed that gardens should be places of beauty and restfulness," characteristics that are evident in the Milliken design.[59] The lot was almost entirely enclosed by thick plantings, with the exception of a narrow entrance off of Park Avenue and openings along the walkway to the north (Fig. 88). Inside the frame of edge planting was a lawn dotted with cherry and dogwood trees. Initially only Seth Milliken and his wife Margaret were buried there, beneath ledger stones by Presbrey-Leland. But eventually separate sites were carved out for the Milliken's daughter and son-in-law, Harold and Margaret Hatch, and for their son, Gerrish, and his family. Farrand added plantings to provide some separation between the three family lots, while maintaining the basic form of this landscape memorial. Farrand, who was well known for her strict requirement that her landscapes be maintained, continued to take an interest in this small lot, at least through the 1940s, visiting the site herself and sending notes to the cemetery's superintendent suggesting pruning, watering, and thinning. Farrand's continuing attention and the interest of the Milliken family may explain why at least some aspects of this landscape survive, while many other planned landscapes have completely disappeared.

Since only remnants of many landscapes remain, the complexity and variety of the individualized landscapes is rarely evident at Woodlawn today. While the landscapes were carefully tended during the lives of the original lot owners or their immediate heirs, maintenance and its attendant expense declined with later generations. The preservation of a healthy designed landscape takes constant maintenance. As plants died, they were not replaced; as they grew, they were not appropriately trimmed. In many cases, Woodlawn's administration was forced to remove plantings when the lots became overgrown or specimen plantings died. The cemetery's administration often corresponded with heirs describing the deteriorated conditions and seeking permission to remove plantings if the lot owner did not choose to deal with the problem. For example, beginning in the fall of 1933, the cemetery's superintendent communicated with an heir of Charles Stickney, noting that overgrown plantings were interfering with surrounding lots and suggesting that practically all plantings be removed from the lot.[60]

This challenge of continuing care and maintenance over generations is evident at two of the most spectacular projects at Woodlawn, both major works of architecture with important landscapes, one of which is entirely lost and the other of which has been recently restored. The Julius Bache mausoleum has been described as "one of the most unique, picturesque and expressive compositions ever attained in an American cemetery."[61] Its circular site close to the Jerome Avenue entrance was purchased by Bache in 1916. The little-known architectural firm of Davis, McGrath & Kiessling designed a diminutive adaptation of Trajan's Kiosk at Philae on the Nile, which was well-known in the early twentieth century from photographs and paintings.[62] As at Philae, massive columns rise above the enclosed structure creating an openwork frame. After its completion, Bache decided to landscape the circle, hiring "landscape engineer" Charles Wellford Leavitt. Leavitt's attention to detail and interest in the "'Old World' styles of Italy, France, and Egypt" and his "mastery of scale and his use of site-specific plantings" was suited to the complexity of the Bache project.[63] Leavitt devised a landscape scheme that would harmonize with the Egyptian-style building (Figs. 89, 90). Having traveled in Egypt, he was familiar with Egyptian plants and landscape, which he attempted to echo by using plants available locally. He had all of the grass removed from the circle, since lawns are not traditional in Egypt, substituting crushed red shale (identified as "sand" on the drawing) in front of the mausoleum and around the plantings. Moss-covered stones led from Linden Avenue to the entrance stairs. Tall cedars, up to forty feet in height, were placed behind the building, with other large evergreen and deciduous plants densely planted on the remainder of the lot, creating one of the most striking juxtapositions of architecture and landscape at the cemetery. Ernest Stevens Leland was ecstatic in his praise:

> Viewed in the twilight of a rubescent sky, this noble Egyptian structure, embraced by verdure rich in reminiscences of the Nile, is a sight which may indeed kindle new reverence for the noble art of landscape design.[64]

Bache lived until 1944 and took a continuing interest in his unoccupied mausoleum and its landscape. However, following his death, maintenance must have declined and the plantings were eventually removed. In place of one of the most imaginative cemetery landscapes of the early twentieth century, the mausoleum is now surrounded by a lawn, which Leavitt had seen as inappropriate for this Egyptian site, with a few scattered shrubs and trees.

Undoubtedly, the finest ensemble of architecture and landscape at Woodlawn is the burial chapel of Edward and Mary Harkness, a masterpiece designed by James Gamble Rogers, beginning in 1923, set in an extensive landscape by Beatrix Farrand (Figs. 91, 92). As superintendent John Plumb

Fig. 89. Julius Bache mausoleum in Whitewood plot, designed circa 1916 by Davis, McGrath & Kiessling and landscaped in an Egyptian style by Charles Wellford Leavitt. *Park and Cemetery* 30 no 12, February 1921, 315. Harvard University. Graduate School of Design. Frances Loeb Library.

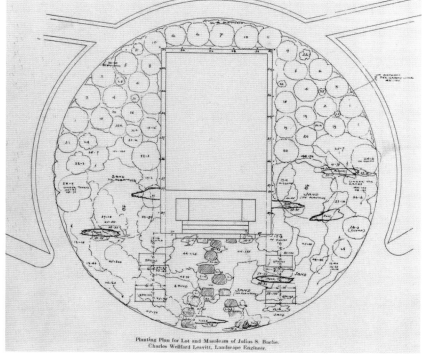

Fig. 90. Charles Wellford Leavitt's planting plan for Julius Bache in Whitewood plot. *Park and Cemetery* 30 no 12, February 1921, 316. Harvard University. Graduate School of Design. Frances Loeb Library.

Fig. 91. English Gothic chapel, designed by James Gamble Rogers in 1923 for Edward Harkness in Golden Rod plot, with landscape by Beatrix Farrand. Photograph by Lee Sandstead.

noted, it was (and is) one of the "show places" of the cemetery.[65] Edward Harkness, heir to a huge fortune inherited from his father, a founder of Standard Oil, spent much of his life distributing his vast wealth to educational and medical institutions. When he donated a building, for example, at Yale, Harvard, and Columbia University Medical Center, Harkness always insisted upon Rogers as the architect. Rogers also designed his house on Fifth Avenue. Rogers designed many of his buildings for Harkness in the Gothic style. For the mausoleum, he created a magnificent miniature English Gothic chapel built of Weymouth granite from Massachusetts, trimmed with Mankato stone from Minnesota. The building is highlighted with ironwork by Samuel Yellin, America's premier iron master, and carving by architectural sculptor Lee Lawrie. The chapel sits at the end of a circular walled garden with paths leading the visitor around the circumference of the circle. A serpentine stone path leads from the road to the garden's roofed, wood and iron entry gate.

Farrand, who designed the landscape at the Harkness's Eolia estate in Waterford, Connecticut (now the Harkness State Park), planned formal plantings with box hedges inside the walls and a more informal planting of trees (white pines, magnolias, dogwoods, cedars, and hemlocks), shrubs (mugho pines, rhododendrons, mountain laurel, and cotoneasters), and ground cover (pachysandra, myrtle, lily of the valley) beyond the walls. For several years after the completion of the project, Farrand and her assistants, Ruth Harvey and Anne Baker, visited the site and wrote regular maintenance reports to the cemetery administration concerning plant care, replanting, thinning of overgrown areas, and other horticultural concerns. Even after Harkness fully turned care over to the cemetery in 1934, Farrand continued commenting on conditions at the site when she was visiting her other Woodlawn projects.[66] But costs rose and Woodlawn could not adequately maintain the aging design of Rogers and Farrand. By 1996, the cemetery reported to the Commonwealth Fund, the organization established by Harkness to continue his philanthropic work, that the garden wall was in very bad shape, the walks needed relaying, and much of the planting needed to be removed. Many of the trees, including some of the white pines, were growing too close to the building, potentially damaging the structure. In 2012, the fund sponsored the restoration of the mausoleum and wall, and replanted the site, adapting Farrand's original conception. As a result, it remains a masterful architecture and landscape ensemble.

Woodlawn Cemetery is an ideal place for the study of both American architecture and landscape. As has long been known and appreciated, major architects, including McKim, Mead & White, Carrère & Hastings, John Russell Pope, and James Gamble Rogers had important commissions at the cemetery. Less well-known and appreciated is the significant role played by the memorialists, the prolific monument companies that, at their best, created impressive mausoleums and smaller-scale memorials that are as beautiful as many of those designed by prestigious architectural firms. Even less well-known is the fact that Woodlawn was an important site of landscapes designed by professional landscape architects who created carefully planned environments that set off the memorials. Probably nowhere else in America could one find landscapes by such important figure in American design as Olmsted Brothers, Beatrix Farrand, Marian Coffin, Ferruccio Vitale, James L. Greenleaf, and Mary Rutherford Jay adjoining one another. To a contemporary visitor, the architecture at Woodlawn still stands out amidst the mature trees that blanket the landscape, but, unfortunately, most of the private landscapes are degraded and await a movement for their restoration. Still, Woodlawn's architectural and landscape design, coupled with its extraordinary sculptures, stained-glass windows, mosaics, and bronze doors, form an artistic ensemble that is among the most complex in the country and remains a physical record of the changing character of American cemeteries over the past 150 years.

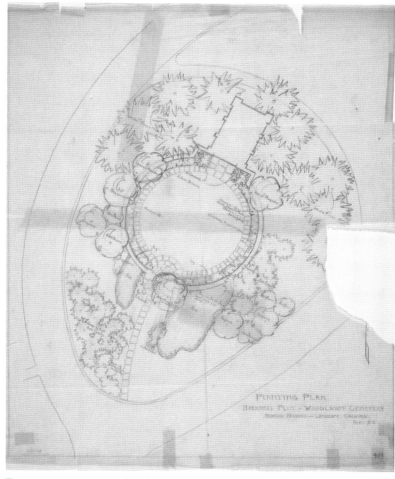

Fig. 92. Beatrix Farrand's planting plan for the garden planned for Edward Harkness in Golden Rod plot. Planting Plan of the Harkness Lot at Woodlawn Cemetery, Beatrix Jones Farrand Collection, Environmental Design Archives, University of California, Berkeley.

1. Ernest Stevens Leland, *The Pioneers of Cemetery Administration in America* (Barre, Vt: privately printed for E. L. Smith & Co., 1941), n.p. The essay on Frederick R. Diering was reprinted from another, unknown source.

2. Aaron Wunsch, "James C. Sidney," in Charles A. Birnbaum and Robin Karson, eds, *Pioneers of American Landscape Design* (New York: McGraw-Hill, 2000), 360-363.

3. At Green-Wood, the architects of a few nineteenth-century monuments and mausoleums have been identified, including Henry Dudley; James Gambrill; Minard Lafever; Detlef Lienau; McKim, Mead & White; George B. Post; Renwick, Aspinwall & Russell; Griffith Thomas; and Richard Upjohn. See Andrew S. Dolkart, "Architecture at Green-Wood," in Jeffrey I. Richman, ed., *Green-Wood at 175: Looking Back/Looking Forward* (Brooklyn: Green-Wood Cemetery, 2012), 67-79.

4. "Local Intelligence: The Homes of the Dead," *New York Times*, March 30, 1866, 2.

5. For an overview of the landscape lawn plan, see David Charles Sloane, *The Last Great Necessity: Cemeteries in American History* (Baltimore: Johns Hopkins University Press, 1991), 99-127.

6. "Woodlawn Cemetery, New York City," *Park and Cemetery* 6, no. 1 (March 1896): 221.

7. *Monumental Work of Robert Caterson* (Bronx: Robert Caterson, 1905).

8. "Some Noted Mausoleums in Woodlawn Cemetery, New York," *Park and Cemetery* 9, no. 8 (October 1899): 172-173.

9. The Gould mausoleum is described in "Woodlawn Cemetery, New York City," *Park and Cemetery* 6, no. 1 (March 1896): 221; Advertising card H.Q. French Memorials, 1897, Woodlawn Cemetery Records, 1863-1999, Drawings & Archives, Avery Architectural & Fine Arts Library, Columbia University (hereafter cited as Woodlawn Cemetery Records). The Warner mausoleum is illustrated in Montgomery Schuyler, "The Work of R.H. Robertson," *Architectural Record* 6 (October-December 1896): 211, where it is mistakenly located in Irvington, N.Y., and in *Inland Architect and News Record* 33, no. 6 (July 1899): plate. This mausoleum was altered on the interior by Cass Gilbert in 1915-16. The Flagler mausoleum is no longer extant. When Flagler moved the family tomb to St. Augustine, he received permission to dismantle the Woodlawn structure. There is no evidence that it was ever re-erected.

10. "Woodlawn Cemetery, New York City," *Park and Cemetery* 6, no. 1 (March 1896): 221.

11. Arthur Bates Jennings designed extensive Queen Anne style alterations to an older house on the northwest corner of Fifth Avenue and West 126th Street for Warner in 1882 and then designed a stable and dwelling at the rear of the lot in 1883 (both demolished). William Tuthill undertook substantial alterations to a commercial building owned by Warner in 1886.

12. William Morrison, "Commercial Buildings," in Mark Alan Hewitt, Kate Lemos, William Morrison, and Charles D. Warren, *Carrère & Hastings Architects*, vol. 1 (New York: Acanthus Press, 2006), 62.

13. Miriam Osborn purchased the Woodlawn plot in 1889, after the death of her husband. However, both she and Charles were initially buried at Green-Wood. In 1893, Norcross Brothers, the construction firm that frequently worked with McKim, Mead & White, applied to Woodlawn for a foundation permit; the mausoleum was completed in 1894. The first entombment is their son Howell Osborn in 1895. Charles and Miriam were moved to Woodlawn in 1902.

14. William Henry Deacy, *Memorials To-day for To-morrow* (Tate, Georgia: Georgia Marble Company, 1928), n.p.

15. Ferdinand Procházka, "Problems of Mausoleum Construction," *Architectural Review* 5 (May 1917): 97.

16. The bronze doors on many mausoleums were equipped with glass insets that could swing open in the summer to provide ventilation.

17. *Book of Presbrey-Leland* (New York: Presbrey-Leland, 1929), plate 15. Monumental stones in a stepped pattern were used on the Woodlawn mausoleum of John H. Flagler, designed by Edward I. Shire, also illustrated on plate 15.

18. Procházka, "Problems of Mausoleum Construction," 97-98.

19. Richard Storms to John Downey of John Downing Building Construction, July 26, 1912, Joseph Milbank major monuments folder, Woodlawn Cemetery Records.

20. R. Storms to James Layng Mills, July 23, 1919, Schoonmaker major monument folder Woodlawn Cemetery Records.

21. *Phillips' Business Directory of New York* (New York: John F. Dwyer, 1909), 673-74.

22. *Farrington Gould and Hoagland, Incorporated: Memorial Designers and Builders: Mausoleums, Monuments, Statuary* (New York: Farrington Gould & Hoagland, Inc., 1927).

23. *Farrington, Gould and Hoagland*, n.p.

24. For the Gates mausoleum, see "Our Costliest Private Mausoleums" *Park and Cemetery* 25, no. 8 (October 1915): 244; John C. Plumb, "Woodlawn Cemetery at New York, *American Landscape Architect* 7 (October 1932): 17. Officially, the Gates mausoleum is the work of the firm of Stone, Gould & Farrington, as the company was known in circa 1910-13.

25. "Presbrey-Land Company," *Park and Cemetery* 30, no. 6 (August 1, 1920): 171. See also the firm's advertisement, *Park and Cemetery* 30, no. 8 (October 1, 1920): 208 and other issues.

26. "The Late W. W. Leland," *Park and Cemetery* 34 (February 1, 1925): 330.

27. *Book of Presbrey-Leland*, 17.

28. "The Late W. W. Leland."

29. In 1922, the Assistant Director of Design was Giles Pollard Greene, who received an architecture degree from Columbia in 1915; see John Marshall Holcombe Jr., ed., *History of the Class of 1911 Yale College,* vol. 3, Decennial Record (New Rochelle: Knickerbocker Press, 1922), 228. The author wishes to thank Matthew J. Kuhnert for providing information on Deacy amassed for a Columbia University paper on one of Deacy's mausoleum designs.

30. *The Book of Presbrey-Leland Memorials* (New York: Presbrey-Leland), 1929, 13.

31. The Heck and Edwards drawings are in the unprocessed Presbrey-Leland Collection, Drawings & Archives, Avery Architectural & Fine Arts library, Columbia University (hereafter cited as Presbrey-Leland Collection).

32. Presbrey-Leland advertisement, *Park and Cemetery* 31 no 6 (August 1, 1921): 162.

33. Advertisement, *Park and Cemetery* 34 no. 3 (May 1, 1924): 68. This ad also appeared in other issues of the journal.

34. *Book of Presbrey-Leland*, 8.

35. "Mausoleums," *Park and Cemetery* 8, no. 11 (January 1899): 218.

36. Presbrey-Leland sketchbook of mausoleums, Presbrey-Leland Collection. This small notebook, with tiny pencil sketches of scores of mausoleums and monuments was probably the property of C.H. Presbrey.

37. *The Book of Presbrey-Leland* (New York: Presbrey-Leland, 1932), 39.

38. William R. Rose major monuments folder, Woodlawn Cemetery Records.

39. "The Twenty-third Annual Exhibition of the Architectural League of New York," *American Architect* 93 (February 12, 1908): 53 and plate; also see Charles D. Warren, "Churches and Tombs," in Hewitt, *Carrère & Hastings Architects*, vol. II, 206-207.

40. "Mrs. John Hubbard, Revised Design for Cemetery Plot at Woodlawn Cemetery," March 29, 1940, Hubbard correspondence file, Woodlawn Cemetery Records. The drawing is signed "Landscape Architect 515 Madison Ave N. Y. C." with no name given. The yellow pages telephone directory from 1940 shows that Flanders was the only landscape

architect at this address. Three photographs by the architectural photography firm of Gottscho-Schleisner, Inc., dated October 8, 1941, are in the collection of the Library of Congress.

41. James Gamble Rogers to Richard Storms, Dec. 13, 1938 and Apr. 20, 1939, Kuhn major monuments folder, Woodlawn Cemetery Records. This monument seems to be largely intact, but is entirely overgrown and difficult to access.

42. Shipman prepared general planting plans as well as a special plan for bulbs, including over a dozen varieties of narcissus.

43. Ernest Stevens Leland, "Planting the Mausoleum Plot, I – The Bache Mausoleum Plot, Charles Wellford Leavitt, Landscape Engineer," *Park and Cemetery* 30, no. 12 (February 1921): 313.

44. See Charles Warren's essay in this volume.

45. Ernest Stevens Leland, "Planting the Mausoleum Plot, IV – The Woolworth Mausoleum," *Park and Cemetery* 32, no. 2 (April 1922): 39.

46. Ernest Stevens Leland, "Planting the Mausoleum Plot, III – The Rhinelander Mausoleum," *Park and Cemetery* 31, no. 9 (November 1, 1921): 239.

47. A few of the trees are extant. Carrère & Hastings also designed the planting around the mausoleum on Henry T. Sloan's circular lot in 1909; this is now the Kavenaugh mausoleum (see H.T. Sloan correspondence folder, Woodlawn Cemetery Records).

48. Mrs. Cass Canfield, letters and report, 1904-05, Records of the Olmsted Associates, Series B, reel 154, no. 3009, Library of Congress.

49. F.L. Olmsted Jr., "Constable Cemetery Lot – Woodlawn," report, September 20, 1905, Records of the Olmsted Associates, Series B, reel 161, no. 3074.

50. Olmsted Brothers to Louise Constable, Jan. 8, 1906, Records of the Olmsted Associates.

51. Olmsted Brothers to W.J. Tompkins, Clerk, Estate of W. A. Constable, Apr. 12, 1912, Records of the Olmsted Associates.

52. A simple landscape plan is extant in the George B. Post correspondence file, Woodlawn Cemetery Records. Only remnants of the landscape survive, including a grove of trees behind the cross, and rhododendrons along the walk at the south border of the lot. For Coffin, see Thaïsa Way, *Unbounded Practice: Women and Landscape Architecture in the Early Twentieth Century* (Charlottesville: University of Virginia Press, 2009), 136-158; Jeanne Marie Teutonico, *Marian Cruger Coffin, the Long Island Estates: A Study of the Early Work of a Pioneering Woman in American Landscape Architecture* (Columbia University, Master's thesis in Historic Preservation, 1983); Valencia Libby "Marian Cruger Coffin," in Birnbaum, *Pioneers of American Landscape Design*, 64-68 and Teutonico, "Marian C. Coffin," in Robert B. MacKay, Anthony Baker and Carol A. Traynor, eds., *Long Island Country Houses and Their Architects 1860-1940* (New York: W. W. Norton and Society for the Preservation of Long Island Antiquities, 1997), 116-118.

53. Stickney correspondence folder, Woodlawn Cemetery Records; the cross is illustrated in Tiffany Studios, Ecclesiastical Department, *Memorials in Glass and Stone* ([New York]: Tiffany Studios, 1922), [54], http://libmma.contentdm.oclc.org/cdm/compoundobject/collection/p16028coll5/id/427/rec/10

54. Percy Pyne major monuments folder, Woodlawn Cemetery Records. For Greenleaf, see Ania Bass, "James L. Greenleaf," in Birnbaum, *Pioneers of American Landscape Design*, 146-149; "Jeanne Marie Teutonico, "James L. Greenleaf," in MacKay, *Long Island Country Houses and Their Architects*, 201-204. For Upton Pyne, see John Turpin and W. Barry Thomson. *New Jersey Country Houses: the Somerset Hills*, vol. I (Far Hills, N.J.: Mountain Colony Press, 2004), 94-99.

55. "Framing the Mausoleum into the Landscape," *Park and Cemetery* 21, no. 2 (April 1, 1911): 522.

56. Leland, "The Woolworth Mausoleum," 40.

57. Trowbridge's surviving partner was Goodhue Livingston. Communications between the architects' office and Woodlawn are signed by firm architect George W. Jacoby; Trowbridge major monuments folder, Woodlawn Cemetery Records.

58. John C. Plumb, Superintendent to Mrs. S. B. P. Trowbridge, Apr. 1, 1949, Trowbridge major monument folder, Woodlawn Cemetery Records. For Vitale, see R. T. Schnadelbach, *Ferruccio Vitale: Landscape Architect of the Country Place Era* (New York: Princeton Architectural Press, 2001); Laurie E. Hempton, "Ferruccio Vitale," in Birnbaum, *Pioneers of Landscape Design*, 417-420; and Wendy Joy Darby, "Vitale & Geiffert," in MacKay, *Long Island Country Houses*, 419-422. Vitale & Geiffert also designed the landscape for Trowbridge's William Porter mausoleum.

59. Diane Kostial McGuire, "Beatrix Farrand's Contribution to the Art of Landscape Architecture," in *Beatrix Jones Farrand (1872-1959): Fifty Years of American Landscape Architecture* (Washington: Dumbarton Oaks, 1982), 34. For Farrand, also see Judith B. Tankard, *Beatrix Farrand: Private Gardens, Public Landscapes* (New York: Monacelli, 2009); Diana Balmori, Diane Kostial McGuire, and Eleanor M. Peck, *Beatrix Farrand's American Landscapes: Her Gardens and Campuses* (Sagaponack, New York: Sagapress, 1985); Peck, "Beatrix Jones Farrand," in Birnbaum, *Pioneers of American Landscape Design*, 117-119; and Balmori, "Beatrix Farrand," in MacKay, *Long Island Country Houses*, 163-165.

60. John C. Plumb to L. Gordon Hamersley, October 25, 1933 and January 17, 1934, Stickney correspondence folder, Woodlawn Cemetery Records.

61. Leland, "The Bache Mausoleum," 314.

62. The only other buildings identified by this firm are two lofts from 1906 (Davis, McGrath & Shepard) and 1911, and the Woodlawn mausoleum for Bache's sister, Henrietta Bache Kayser (1920-21).

63. Heidi Hohmann, "Charles Wellford Leavitt, Jr.," in Birnbaum, *Pioneers of American Landscape Design*, 224.

64. Leland, "Bache Mausoleum," 315.

65. Beatrix Farrand to John C. Plumb, Mar. 1933, Edward Harkness major monuments folder, Woodlawn Cemetery Records.

66. Farrand to Plumb, Nov. 6, 1934, Edward Harkness major monuments folder, Woodlawn Cemetery Records.

W.F. HAVEMEYER

SCULPTED MEMORIALS:
TRADITION AND INNOVATION

CYNTHIA MILLS

Angels and crosses, mourning women, portrait busts, sphinxes, and modernist experiments. Cemetery managers have encouraged variety and sober innovation in the selection of sculptural memorials erected at Woodlawn. Although styles, themes, and materials have changed since the cemetery's founding in the 1863, this goal has been maintained over a century and a half, resulting in a landscape that features an array of monuments – some made by celebrated fine artists – and a distinctive identity. The figure of a sleeping babe was the first sculpture installed in Woodlawn Cemetery. On a slope at the northeast corner, this small child fashioned from white marble rests peacefully in death, clutching a lily of the valley in his left hand. With eyes closed and head slightly turned on a sculpted pillow, his right hand rests on his chest over his loose gown. He crosses one chubby barefoot leg over the other in a display of innocence intended to pull at the heartstrings of nineteenth-century viewers. The inscription on the sarcophagus below mourns one-year-old Caleb Brinthall Knevals, who died on March 23, 1865. Bolt holes next to the stone mattress indicate the figure was originally covered with a glass case to protect the porous marble from the effects of wintry weather and precipitation. This tiny sculpture is an apt symbol of the melancholy sentimentality predominant in the pre-Civil War "rural" cemeteries, the initial model for Woodlawn's founders (Fig. 93).

Other early works can be found a few steps away. Just across the path stands the "cushioned desk and open Bible in Mr. James Hall's lot" which the cemetery's report for the year of 1867 noted, "attract great attention" and "are much admired." While many families installed "ordinary headstones and footstones" that year, the report continued, "it is gratifying to note that several new devices have been introduced which are at once novel, appropriate and tasteful."[1] The outsized book and the mammoth cushion beneath it, decorated with ropes and swags, demonstrate a carver's love of recreating the qualities of different materials, such as the ephemeral softness of cloth and the fineness of paper, in Tuckahoe marble. Family records were often kept in Bibles, and here the pages of the book are filled with the names and life dates of those who have died, with verses memorializing them. The family name HALL appears on the back of the pedestal in raised Gothic-style lettering, much as it might appear on the leather cover of the family Bible (Fig. 94).

The identities of the makers of the Knevals baby and the Hall Bible are now lost to us. Over the ensuing decades, a number of monument companies opened works adjacent to Woodlawn Cemetery; survivors could go there or to the firms' Manhattan showrooms to select memorials

PLATE 3. Havemeyer monument in Beech plot. Photograph by Gavin Ashworth.

SCULPTED MEMORIALS   91

Fig. 93. The first sculpture at Woodlawn is located in Spring Lake plot. It is a memorial to Caleb B. Knevals, the infant son of one of the cemetery's founders. Photograph by Gavin Ashworth.

Fig. 94. Prominently located near the entrance to the cemetery in Chapel Hill plot, the Hall monument overlooks the Bronx River Valley. Photograph by Gavin Ashworth.

for their loved ones in face-to-face transactions with dealers, some of whom also acted as intermediaries for Italian exporters. The seated woman marking J.F. Underhill's nearby lot, for example, is described in the 1867 annual report as an "Italian Marble Statue."[2] She looks upward to heaven, holding flowers in her lap. A short distance away, the memorial honoring James A. Edgar, who died in 1867, is another beatific female figure. She stands looking up to the sky as she grips a stone cross. Such monuments participated in the period interest in using symbolic references, such as flowers representing purity and the fleeting beauty of life, ship's anchors representing hope, and Christian crosses speaking of faith that the departed have gone on to a new home in Heaven.

Monumental Sculpture

While the cemetery's founding coincided with the Civil War, relatively few of its monuments focus directly on that conflict. The most important is the grave of Admiral David Glasgow Farragut, the Union naval hero, which became the focus of annual commemorative events. More than 10,000 soldiers and sailors joined by President Ulysses S. Grant marched on October 1, 1870 in a funeral procession two miles long to deliver Farragut's body to Woodlawn Cemetery, with the final leg of the journey on the New York and Harlem Railroad. The monument, commissioned by Farragut's wife, Virginia, and son, Loyall, is a white marble column in the form of a broken ship's mast, draped with an American flag and decorated with military emblems: an anchor and rope, three shields, including one bearing the image of his flagship the *Hartford*, a compass, block and tackle, and sword. The monument is located in the Aurora Hill plot on Woodlawn's first circular mound, donated by the cemetery in honor of Farragut's achievements; it attracted new public attention to Woodlawn. It was made by the firm of Casoni and Isola, which had a shop on Broadway and imported marble from quarries in Carrara, Italy.[3] (Fig. 95) (see Fig. 18)

White marble bore an association with purity and with classical sculpture, but it is also porous and easily degradable. Many cemeteries began to discourage its use as American granite quarries developed in the late nineteenth century and new technologies, such as steam-powered tools, came into use allowing carvers to work more easily in harder stone such as granite (which could be highly polished). Woodlawn always permitted the use of marble.

The emphasis on high-quality, custom monuments was only strengthened when the cemetery began shifting to a "landscape lawn" plan in the late 1860s in undeveloped sections. This newer aesthetic eliminated visible boundaries, such as hedges and copings, between plots and favored creation of broad vistas enhanced by fewer, more artistic monuments (one family monument per lot) whose attractive qualities could be shared by all. The emphasis was on using monuments to create a special place full of beauty – a response to the growing clutter of markers found in many of the earlier "rural" cemeteries. Cemetery managers advised survivors to heed the words of landscape designer Adolph Strauch, whose work at Spring Grove Cemetery in Cincinnati was a model for the reform landscape aesthetic. Strauch warned that the bereaved, not knowing what to do, often spent money willy-nilly on a too-numerous collection of gravestones for their lots without considering the general effect. "Instead of the multiplication of cheap and common pieces, the mere work of the stone-cutter," he wrote in 1867, "it would be far better to put money into something which, for its massiveness or its artistic excellence, would be a testimonial in favor of the erection. Those who have monuments to erect, should wait until they can avail themselves of the advice of persons of taste, and thereby make a real addition to the attractions of the place, in whose beauty so many have an interest."[4]

Strauch's words reflected a view of fine art sculpture that preceded by several decades the shift in taste to monuments made by French-trained sculptors and architects that peaked from the turn of the century to the years after World War I. Throughout Woodlawn's history most monuments continued to be ornamental stone figures that were imported or made by American monument companies. Thus most are not attributed to any specific artist. These could be selected from design books, but the companies also retained sculptors capable of composing their own artistic designs. The two pages of names of monument dealers and construction firms that are listed in a cemetery ledger book testify to their diversity and the combination of artistry and commercialism they represent.[5]

Mourning female figures continued to be a major theme in the 1870s and 1880s as well as winged angels. One outstanding example was the Andrew Foster Smith memorial in Spring Lake plot, designed by Italian sculptor Giovanni Maria Benzoni, whose name remains on the base along with the year, 1872. Benzoni produced a vast array of sculpture, much of it for export, at his studios in Rome and died only one year after this sculpture was completed. It shows an earnest young girl with flowing tresses kneeling on the bow of a boat, with anchor chains and waves at its base. She holds a cross to her chest and looks forward in hope and faith in the hereafter. The stone base below appears to have been made by the Casoni and Isola firm, and the whole ensemble exemplifies the transfer of technique, material, and artistic ideas from Italy to New York in this era. It features two bas reliefs: a cross and lilies on one side and an angel on the other, its foot resting upon the clouds and one arm elevated. The inscription honors "Andrew Foster, only son," and notes that he died in Rome, which had been an aesthetic beacon and home to such American artists as Thomas Crawford and Randolph Rogers (Fig. 96).

Fig. 95. The monument to Admiral David Glasgow Farragut by Cassoni and Isola is located at the center of Woodlawn's first well defined circular lot in Aurora Hill plot. Photograph by Lee Sandstead.

Fig. 96. The Andrew Foster Smith monument, located in Spring Lake plot, was designed and produced in the Rome studio of Giovanni Maria Benzoni. Photograph by Lee Sandstead.

While the Smith memorial has a human scale, the William Frederick Havemeyer memorial is a colossal work elevated high above the viewer. A stone sculpture of a woman, her hand to her chin in the age-old symbol of meditation and melancholy, she wears a loose gown, whose folds fall in straight lines adding to the impression that she is like an enduring pillar, and she holds a memorial wreath (Fig. 97) (see Fig. 30). This is one of the memorials at Woodlawn that are the product of the New England Granite Company, where the Prussian-born, Munich-trained sculptor Carl Conrads reigned from 1866-1903 as the primary sculptor. The artist had served as a Union artilleryman in the Civil War before beginning his American career with the Hartford-based firm. Later he went on to solid success producing many Civil War monuments and two statues for the U.S. Capitol's National Statuary Hall, as well as other funerary work. New England Granite would make numerous works in Woodlawn including the George Pancoast memorial.[6]

Fig. 97. A sculpture by Carl Conrads atop a column by New England Granite Co. stands at the center of the circular Havemeyer lot in Beech plot. Photograph by Lee Sandstead.

The 1886 family monument of conductor Leopold Damrosch, who founded the Oratorio Society of New York and led the Metropolitan Opera in his final year, is the last great work of German sculptor Friedrich Traugott Helbig. A woman wearing a cloak over her head sits on a claw-footed throne with a regal air, evincing the majesty of an operatic star on stage. She holds what appear to be oak leaves in one hand. Her long gown slips from one shoulder and flows below her in curving folds. Below, the name DAMROSCH declares whose memorial this is in bold capital letters. A lyre (now lost) and foliage at the base completed the presentation. The monument was erected by the Oratorio, Arion, and Symphony Societies of New York (Fig. 98).

Simplicity may sometimes be deceiving as we gauge the importance of early memorials. Erastus Dow Palmer designed a flaming urn, executed in granite for the Hurtt memorial (1884) in Cypress plot. The stone urn, which stands atop a cylindrical column with a border of decorative leaves at the top is an elegant summation of funerary traditions of the classical world.[7] Palmer was an influential designer of cemetery sculpture who lived and worked in Albany, New York, where one of his best-known works is his *Angel at the Sepulchre* created for the Albany Rural Cemetery.

Sculptors sometimes honored fellow sculptors in this period with bronze bas relief-portraits and stone busts. Henry Baerer, a Munich-born artist, designed a profile bas-relief portrait in bronze of his teacher, the well-known sculptor Robert Launitz for his memorial in 1871. Launitz (1806-1870) who was born in Latvia and trained in Italy, had gained renown in part by designing a number

of marble monuments for American cemeteries, including Brooklyn's Green-Wood; he was also a mentor to and employer of foreign artists arriving in the United States. Baerer is perhaps best known for his sculpture of Beethoven in Central Park.

Caspar Buberl, an immigrant from Bohemia, who had also studied with Launitz, designed a bust of the bearded artist Ernst Plassmann (1823-1877), signed and dated 1879 on one shoulder (Fig. 99). Plassmann was a German-born sculptor and woodcarver who had established Plassmann's School of Art in New York City. He was best known for his figure of Tammany for Tammany Hall (1869) and his statue of Benjamin Franklin (1872) on Park Row. Plassmann is shown as a universal man, without indication of contemporary clothing, his hair swept back to give him a sense of power and intelligence. According to the *American Art Review*, "a concert, promoted, by the New York German Society of Art and Science, held Nov. 4, 1880, and private contributions, realized adequate funds" for the bust placed on a granite pedestal.[8]

The sculpture on the monument to interior designer Auguste Pottier made by French sculptor Frédéric Bartholdi, who later designed the Statue of Liberty, has been lost, but a diagram by a cemetery foreman survives and shows the figure that has been removed.[9] What remains is the impressive granite pedestal bearing an oval bronze bas relief of Pottier from 1881. Pottier, a native of France, whose firm Pottier and Stymus designed and built furniture and interiors for some of the wealthiest families in America, is shown in formal dress facing in three-quarter view within an oval frame (Fig. 100).

Fig. 99. Caspar Buberl's bust of fellow sculptor Ernst Plassmann located in North Border plot. Photograph by Lee Sandstead.

Fig. 100. Frédéric Auguste Bartholdi's bronze figure *Grief* is missing from the granite pedestal of the Pottier memorial in Aurora Hill plot. Photograph by Gavin Ashworth.

The technical sophistication of American bronze foundries increased rapidly, and as Beaux-Arts trained American sculptors emerged after the 1870s, the taste for modeling in clay and casting in bronze grew in New York. Modeling in clay allowed the design of more fluid, naturalistic figures than those made from carved stone. American enterprises such as Jno. Williams, Inc. and Henry-Bonnard Bronze Company made the city an important site for artistic bronze casting. At the end of the century, New York became the center of the American art world with arts academies and museums providing means for the training of American artists and exhibition of artworks. At the same time, sculpture for cemeteries was elevated in the hierarchy of art and was sometimes displayed in art galleries as well as in the graveyard. Virtually all of the nation's most famous artists made works for cemeteries and this proved to be a golden age for sculpture at Woodlawn.

Two of Woodlawn's most beautiful bronze figures are the work of William Ordway Partridge (1861-1930), a cosmopolitan artist and erudite writer and lecturer who also had a brief career as an actor. Partridge could be considered a member of the second generation of Beaux-Arts sculptors, along with Philip Martiny and Adolph Weinman. He made realistic portraits but also some symbolic works, including several for American cemeteries. Partridge's Samuel Hay Kauffman memorial (1897), an idealized female figure of Memory sitting on a Grecian-inspired exedra and contemplating a wreath, in the Rock Creek Cemetery, in Washington, D.C., is among the most important ones that preceded his works at Woodlawn.

Partridge worked with architect Duncan Candler to create the Woodlawn memorial for Joseph

Pulitzer, the publisher of the *New York World* and *St. Louis Post-Dispatch* newspapers who died suddenly of heart disease aboard his yacht *Liberty* in 1911. After his death, authorities estimated his estate to be worth nearly $20 million. The monument Partridge designed is an idealized male figure in bronze, perhaps representing memory, meditation, or mourning, or a combination of these symbolic attributes. Seated on a severely plain granite throne, he holds an urn in his right hand and turns his head to contemplate it. He raises his left hand to his head in a gesture suggesting thoughtful questioning. A narrow strap across his bare chest connects drapery that falls back from his right shoulder like a cloak to the portion of the voluminous garment laid over his lap. The setting appears to have been simplified from an original design. Plans in the Woodlawn archive at Avery Library, show that a higher stele behind the figure had once been envisioned with a beribboned garland encircling the figure's head and shoulders, like an aureole. Large bird wings demarcated the ends of the benches in this early design, much like the bench of the famed Adams Memorial (1891) in the Rock Creek Cemetery, Washington, D.C., designed by Augustus Saint-Gaudens, who worked with architect Stanford White to create influential settings and figures that combined naturalistic elements, the ideal, and the decorative. The Pulitzer memorial's architectural setting is a sparer one, stripped of most decoration except for a delicate classical molding. With its symmetrical curving benches, it provides a white background in high-quality Barre granite for the dark metal figure that is enhanced at certain times of day by the play of light and shadow.

The Pulitzer monument was pictured on the cover of *Monumental News*, a magazine of the memorial industry, in January 1916, where it was described as "one of the finest of modern types of the architectural exedra memorials" and "a rarely dignified and impressive memorial." The magazine also praised Partridge for rendering "a figure of rare sculptural expression and monumental feeling."[10] (Fig. 101)

Another monument by Partridge, more emotional in tenor, commemorates six of the lives lost

Fig. 101. The bronze sculpture by William Ordway Partridge in a setting designed by architect Duncan Candler memorializes Joseph Pulitzer in Evergreen plot. Avery Library, Drawings & Archives, Woodlawn Cemetery Records.

in a tragic fire on April 7, 1899, at the Fifth Avenue mansion of millionaire New York businessman Wallace Corodon Andrews. Wallace, president of the New York Steam Heating Company, and his wife Margaret perished in the blaze along with her sister-in-law Georgiana St. John and Mrs. St. John's three children as well as several servants. Partridge designed a female figure clad in a freely flowing robe with a headdress that perhaps summons up biblical times. She appears to be beckoning, as she reaches forward, her back foot rising from the ground. Or perhaps she is meant to be praying. Partridge again worked with architect Candler on this project, and the sculpture is placed on a low granite base with the name ANDREWS incised at the bottom. A bronze plaque on the back of the base lists the names of the family members who died in the fire (Fig. 102). Partridge appears to have gained the confidence of the trustee of the estate, Gamaliel St. John, to prepare the memorial more than a decade after the deaths.

Artist Philip Martiny, once a key assistant to Saint-Gaudens, created the figure of Jesus Christ for the Gulbenkian tomb in a setting designed by architect William H. Deacy, which marks the graves of two men who were murdered in 1918 (Fig. 103). The victims were Gullabi Gulbenkian, an Armenian rug merchant, and his nephew Serope, both fatally shot by a longtime employee at their business on Fifth Avenue. The accused was later judged insane and pardoned from his death sentence by the governor.[11] Martiny, who came to the United States from his native France at the age of 20, was a prolific sculptor whose work the famed sculptor Daniel Chester French once wrote, had "style" and a "distinguished quality."[12] He produced myriad public commissions of great variety. The Gulbenkian monument was one of his later works, completed just two years before he suffered a paralyzing stroke in 1921 that ended his career. It shows the bronze Christ standing hands outstretched between two pairs of Doric columns in a temple-like structure that *Monumental News* said may evoke the non-Christian classical world. "This introduction of the Savior against a structure of pure pagan art might jar the sensibilities of those who fail to find a subtle symbolism suggested by the triumph of Christianity over paganism," the writer commented, then added, "Whatever motifs may have inspired the patron to thus blend two opposite themes, the fact remains that as an abstract composition in design the ensemble is admirable, impressive and stately."[13] The cemetery managers found the monument appealing enough to include it as the first plate in their promotional book of cemetery views published in 1925.[14]

One of the most unusual monuments at Woodlawn of its era is the Clarence Emerson Wheeler memorial (1887), a low relief – like a painting in bronze – attached to the face of a colossal boulder. The picture shows a youth, perhaps intended to represent Clarence, who died at age 13, lying

Fig. 102. The St. John / Andrews monument in Oak Hill plot, designed by architect Duncan Candler, includes William Ordway Partridge's bronze figure standing on a low pedestal. Photograph by Gavin Ashworth.

Fig. 103. Architect William H. Deacy designed the setting for a bronze figure by Philip Martiny memorializing the Gulbenkian family in Chestnut Hill plot. Avery Library, Drawings & Archives, Presbrey-Leland collection.

in a grassy field absorbed in reading a book (Fig. 104). He appears lost in the imaginary world of a novel that takes one to another realm, like a dreamland. He wears contemporary boy's clothing including knee breeches. His face and back are drawn clearly with long contour lines. In the grass, which seems loosely sketched in, we see flowers, including daisies and one rose, which add to the sense of his innocence and the delicate melancholy of the whole scene. The sculptor James Edward Kelly (1855-1933) had been an illustrator in his youth for *Harper's* and *Scribner's* magazines; he knew and admired the artist Winslow Homer and was a friend of Edwin Austin Abbey. The figure of the young boy evokes a similar sentiment to Homer's watercolor *The New Novel* (1877) at the Museum of Fine Arts, Springfield, Massachusetts. Later Kelly went on to fame as a sculptor of war memorials. The monument was commissioned by Jerome B. Wheeler, Clarence Wheeler's father. Jerome Wheeler, whose family claimed a distant connection to Ralph Waldo Emerson, was a co-owner of Macy's Department Stores, a successful silver mine owner, and a founder of Aspen, Colorado.

Over the decades, major sculptors continued to work in stone as well as bronze. Daniel Chester French, who after Saint-Gaudens's death became America's leading sculptor, during a long and productive career, in 1911 contributed the figure of a stone angel sitting at a tomb decorated with flowers (Fig.105). The angel turns in apparent surprise; one hand with fingers open touches the low tomb with a kind of caress, the other with its fingers closed. The angel's wings are spread open, its toes pressed to the ground prepared to rise. The setting is hollowed out beneath a curving architrave to suggest the idea of a cave or tomb, akin to the place where Christ's body was laid before the resurrection. French was one of the great makers of angels in the late nineteenth- and early twentieth-centuries and a master of relief sculpture. Note how the angel's right wing is partially in low relief, while the left wing projects nearly free of the back wall, as the figure turns. The artist's most famous angelic figure is *The Angel of*

Fig. 104. The bronze bas relief memorial to Clarence Emerson Wheeler by James Edward Kelly is located in Cypress plot. Photograph by Gavin Ashworth.

Fig. 105. Sculptor Daniel Chester French's figure was carved by the Piccirilli brothers for a setting designed by architect Henry Bacon. The Kinsley monument is located in Hawthorn plot. Avery Library, Drawings & Archives, Woodlawn Cemetery Records.

Death and the Sculptor for Boston's Forest Hills Cemetery, a version of which is in the collection of the Metropolitan Museum of Art.

French's Woodlawn figure marks the grave of Herbert M. Kinsley, a Chicago restaurateur who had, in his later years, become one of the proprietors of the elegant new Holland House hotel in New York City. Newspaper accounts said he died under the surgeon's knife in September 1894 after seeking treatment for a long-standing health problem.[15] Kinsley had three daughters. One daughter married Charles Hutchinson of Chicago, and perhaps she and her husband were initiators of the memorial, for French's account book listed the project under the name "Hutchinson" at $8,230.50. The name KINSLEY is incised on the base of the memorial, and the sculptor's name, D C French 1911, is discreetly incised on the stone beneath the tomb. A low bench is provided nearby for contemplation of the monument.[16]

Augustus Lukeman, who had been a student of French's, also designed a stone angel for Woodlawn, a relief sculpture for the Anderson memorial in Cypress plot. His angel spreads its great wings and turns its cloaked profile in meditation. Arms rest lithesomely on one propped-up leg, while the other is stretched out. The drapery is comprised of almost abstract curving lines. Lukeman, a Virginian born in 1872, had made numerous Civil War memorials as well as work for cemeteries, such as a seated female tomb sculpture he exhibited at the 1898 National Sculpture Society exhibition in New York.[17] Another important angel is found in Adolph Weinman's Wolcott memorial (1906), accompanying a monument by McKim, Mead & White in the Parkview plot, the kneeling child angel rests its praying hands on a shield bearing a cross. It marks the grave of Edward Oliver Wolcott, a U.S. senator from Colorado.

Fig. 106. *The Outcast* by Attilio Piccirilli in Myostosis plot. Photograph by Lee Sandstead.

Sculptors often worked repeatedly with the same architects and carvers, with whom they found a harmonious relationship. French worked with architect Henry Bacon, a frequent partner, on the Kinsley memorial and arranged for it to be carved by Piccirilli studios, which executed almost all his work in stone.

In fact, the six Piccirilli brothers, a Bronx-based family of stone carvers, left a major imprint on the cemetery. They executed a number of designs by leading sculptors, including, for example, Robert Aitken's Bliss memorial at Woodlawn. Sculptors usually fashioned their work in clay and then sent them in the form of plaster casts to the Piccirillis for transformation into stone. During their careers the brothers carved such iconic works as French's statue of Abraham Lincoln for the Lincoln Memorial in Washington and the lions by Edward Clark Potter in front of the New York Public Library.

Attilio Piccirilli was a sculptor as well as a carver, who designed his own award-winning compositions, three of which are represented at Woodlawn. *The Outcast* (1908) (Fig. 106) is a nude male figure seated upon a rock that summons up Jean-Baptiste Carpeaux's moving *Ugolino* (1862) in its expression of personal torment or Rodin's *The Thinker* for his *Gates of Hell*. Critics noted the way the figure's physical and emotional malaise was expressed by its clutching, nearly clawing, fingers and toes, one foot tensely pressing against the other in agony. It attracted crowds in 1915 at the Panama-Pacific International Exposition in San Francisco where it won a gold medal, and again was given a prominent position at the 1916 sculpture exhibition in Buffalo.[18] One version (since lost) went to St. Mark's-in-the-Bouwerie and a second remained in the artist's collection until his death in 1945; presumably that is the one installed at Woodlawn in 1947 to mark the grave of his nephew Nathan Piccirilli, a young ensign who was killed in World War II.

Attilio Piccirilli, who had trained at the Accademia di San Luca in Rome, was perhaps best known for his 1913 Maine Monument at the corner of Central Park. Designed by H. Van Buren Magonigle – a frequent collaborator – the monument commemorates the deaths of 260 American sailors in the explosion of the battleship *Maine* in Havana, Cuba, in 1898. One of the most moving groups on that monument depicts a mother comforting a grieving child; Piccirilli also exhibited versions of that group separately as *Fortitude* or *Mater Amoroso*. A bronze cast of it was installed in the cemetery in 1926 as the Piccirilli Family memorial, and a stone version was later placed in the cemetery in 1947 as the DeBlasio memorial (Fig. 107). The mother envelops the child with her caring gestures. The gentle way in which her hands touch the child's leg and torso and the simple direct fashion in which the child rubs his eyes in sorrow, carry a significant part of the emotional message calling for our empathy. The child's nudity suggests its innocence and universality, purity in a world of great difficulty.

Attilio Piccirilli became a friend of New York Mayor Fiorello La Guardia and his family, and designed a memorial at Woodlawn for La Guardia's first wife, Thea, that says much about their close relationship. Piccirilli had given the La Guardias a bronze statuette of a child, entitled *The First Step*, as a wedding gift; it showed a child struggling to walk for the first time without assistance. When Mrs. La Guardia and the couple's one-year-old daughter Fioretta died within a few months' time of each other, the sculptor returned to this theme for his memorial, originally a stone relief and later cast into bronze (Fig. 108). The child and mother are portrayed in an idyllic field, with lilies at right; the mother has collected other flowers, possibly long-stemmed roses, which rest in her lap. The child takes a hesitating step, arms forward to balance herself. She reaches out to her mother who waits ready to sweep the babe securely into her arms. The names Thea and Fioretta appear with no further elaboration in the upper left corner of the relief.[19] Biographer Josef Vincent Lombardo describes the overall effect as highly decorative in its expression of "a gentle sentiment."[20] Mayor La Guardia wrote the preface to Lombardo's biography of Attilio Piccirilli.

Fig. 107. *Mater Amorosa* by Attilio Piccirilli. The bronze cast memorializes the Piccirilli family in Rose Hill plot; another version, carved in stone, is placed in Woodlawn for the De Blasio family memorial. Photograph by Lee Sandstead.

Sculpture for Mausoleums

Woodlawn is distinctive for its wealth and diversity of mausoleums, and sculptors found considerable work contributing doors and other architectural reliefs as well as sphinxes and lions to ornament these houses of the dead. The sculptors were most often subcontractors working with the architects commissioned to make the mausoleums, but occasionally they signed agreements made directly with the patrons.

Following in the long tradition of Italian, French and German cemetery designs, the doors are often reliefs of standing figures, sometimes seen from the side or rear view with face obscured so that the viewer can substitute his or her own emotions. The figures are often framed by the grill, a background of organic or abstract shapes, which allows ventilation from the interior.

The mausoleum door marks the protective entrance to the realm of the dead, with entrance blocked to all but the closest family members. One of the most exceptional of these doors at Woodlawn is the low relief depicting a woman in flowing garments that artist Paul Wayland Bartlett made for William A. Clark (Fig. 109). Clark, who had made a fortune in banking, mining, and railroads, and later served as U.S. senator from Montana, began planning his mausoleum after the March 1893 death of his wife, Katherine Stauffer. The viewer must approach to make out the shadowy figure with a sad expression and cloaked head gently leaning to one side. The composition for the door, titled

Fig. 108. Attilio Piccirilli's memorial to Fiorello La Guardia's wife Thea and young daughter Fioretta. Photograph by Gavin Ashworth.

The Vision, was described by critic Charles de Kay of the *New York Times* as combining gestures of "modesty and appeal" as "the abundant draperies and the right hand raised to the breast furnish at once a suggestion of modesty and offer a gesture that calls attention to the person represented; in other words, it is an appeal to be remembered by the living." De Kay noted that the border of large poppies, representing sleep, in contrasting high relief, creates a heavy frame that adds to the ghostlike quality of the figure.[21] Bartlett had studied the borders of cathedral doors in Italy and photographs of poppy-like plants. He labored on the Clark commission in his studio in Paris but, unusually for an expatriate artist, he had the relief and three border panels cast at one of the new American-based foundries, the Henry-Bonnard Bronze Company in New York (managed by a Frenchman) in late 1897. Bartlett was deeply interested in the history of bronze casting and, according to scholar Michael Shapiro, revived an older method in this project: "The border for the doorway is the first known lost-wax [cire perdue] casting by the Henry-Bonnard foundry and one of the first to be cast in America."[22]

Figures like Bartlett's *Vision* were usually developed from drawings and models. A photograph shows that the French-trained Bartlett, true to Beaux-Arts methods, first made a small nude figure in the round in the pose he wanted for the door, and then referred to it in completing the full-sized clay model of the relief within the already-designed border.[23] It was apparently never intended to be a portrait of Mrs. Clark, as Clark wrote in a letter to the artist, "I note that there is no effort made to incorporate the profile of Mrs. Clark in the figure."[24] Bartlett placed his name on the bottom frame of the door. At about the same time, Bartlett completed his figures of Columbus and Michelangelo for the Library of Congress reading room in Washington D.C. He later designed the pediment for the House wing of the U.S. Capitol (1908-1916), and an equestrian Lafayette presented to the French nation on behalf of the American people.

Another significant door is the entry to the Gates mausoleum created in 1914 by Robert Ingersoll Aitken, a California-born sculptor who had trained in Paris and taught at the National Academy in New York. Aitken's flowing figure of a grieving woman, seen from the rear with drapery slipping down to reveal a long and sinuous form, is a play of curved and angular contour lines (Fig. 110). Her long fingers speak of the tension between her continuing agony at her loved one's absence, as seen in the clawing motion of her right hand and her need for calm reflection and endurance in the left hand. Her head is bowed and her face hidden from our view signifying the ravages grief works on the harmony and beauty of the human face. Aitken signed his name below. He exhibited the model

Fig. 109. The door of the Clark Mausoleum in Oak Hill plot was sculpted by Paul Wayland Bartlett and cast at the Henry-Bonnard foundry. The façade of the mausoleum is a scaled down version of the design by the French architect Henri Deglane. Photograph by Gavin Ashworth.

Fig. 110. The door of the Gates mausoleum in Pine plot by sculptor Robert Aitken. Avery Library, Drawings & Archives, Woodlawn Cemetery Records.

Fig. III. Adolph Weinman's bas relief overdoor panel for the Leeds mausoleum, by architect John Russell Pope, in Walnut plot. Photograph by Lee Sandstead.

for this piece and it was illustrated several times, including on the first page of an essay about Aitken in *The International Studio* in 1913.[25]

Adolph Weinman's relief panel above the entrance to the Leeds mausoleum was also pictured on the first page of an article entitled "A Higher Quality in Funerary Monuments" that appeared in the *American Architect* magazine, thereby promoting fine-art trends in the cemetery (Fig. III). Author William Walton noted that it depicts allegories of "Silence, with a string-less harp, and Memory, with urn and veil."[26]

A number of Italian-born immigrant sculptors specialized in funerary work, and contributed doors to Woodlawn's array of mausoleums. They may have made connections with architects building these mausoleums through such associations as the Architectural League of New York where models for doors and other decorative reliefs were annually shown, as well as through the National Sculpture Society. James Novelli, for example, born in Sulmona, Italy, in 1885, raised in New York City's Little Italy and graduated from the Royal Academy of Rome in 1908, is responsible for at least four mausoleum doors: the Rowan mausoleum angels of 1901, and Beer, Schmuck and Lowenstein mausoleums in the 1920s. Several of these were exhibited at the annual Architectural League shows, as was his free-standing bronze figure of a woman mourner for the Thomas James Stewart memorial, completed in 1923.[27]

Gaetano Federici, who arrived in the United States as an infant and worked in Paterson, New Jersey, designed the Nauss and Wallace mausoleum doors as well as the arched Seibert mausoleum entrance, with its lovely grill of floral and abstract shapes, completed in 1928 (Fig. 112). He had trained entirely in America with a number of different sculptors, including Giuseppe Moretti, Charles Henry Niehaus, Karl Bitter, and William Ordway Partridge, combining his own ideas of the baroque with their Beaux-Arts ideals. His *Spirit of the Resurrection* (1936) in Laurel Grove Memorial Park, Totowa, New Jersey, is his most famous memorial sculpture.[28]

Oronzio Maldarelli, born in Naples to the family of a goldsmith, also arrived in the United States as a child and was educated in New York. He designed the melancholy figure on the door of the J.C. Penney mausoleum (1929). A graceful circle of foliage comprises the grill surrounding her head like a halo. His name appears on the lower right hand corner of the door.

At times, sculptors contributed elaborate relief sculptures to the facades of mausoleums, working closely with architects on such projects. New York sculptor Edward Sanford's design of barefoot figures in an apparent funeral procession, their garments falling in straight lines, on the Garvan mausoleum (1927), designed by architect John Russell Pope, is an important example (Fig. 113). Oscar Lenz's beautiful panels of angels, the gentle recording female angel and the muscular male angel, for the Thomas Mason mausoleum (1899) are cleanly and clearly drawn in low relief. The Latin phrases *Ab Initio, Ad Finem* ("from beginning to end") and *Sic Transit Gloria Mundi* ("thus passes away the glory of the world") accompany the figures.

Egyptian themes inspired mausoleum doors, such as the one designed by Julius Loester for the Woolworth mausoleum, with costume, birds, and flowers intended to signify ancient Egypt and its enduring mysteries. The sculptor of the sphinxes on the monument has not been definitively identified (Fig. 114). However, considerable documentation remains about the granite lions that J. Massey Rhind created for the Ehret mausoleum. A 1901 agreement with the patron, a German-born brewer, specified that the final lions would be based on models presented by the sculptor and stated that "the entire execution [was] to be of highest artistic merit, and first class in every respect" in exchange for payment of $4,000.[29] (Fig. 115) Rhind, who trained in Scotland and France, completed significant architectural sculptures, including figures for the Grant Memorial. The Ehret lions are muscular creatures, but in each case, one front paw tenderly rests upon the other in a gesture of somber respect.

Sometimes mausoleum doors could be added or changed over the years, as in the tomb of railroad baron Collis Huntington. A door by

Fig. 112. Door of the Siebert mausoleum in Parkview plot by Gaetano Federici. Photograph by Lee Sandstead.

Fig. 113. Bronze patinated panels by Edward Sanford flank the door of the Garvan mausoleum, by architect John Russell Pope, in Myostosis plot. Photograph by Gavin Ashworth.

Fig. 114. Stone sphinxes by an unidentified sculptor flank the doors of the Woolworth mausoleum by the monument company Farrington, Gould & Hoagland in Pine plot. Avery Library, Drawings & Archives, Woodlawn Cemetery Records.

Fig. 115. Lions by J. Massey Rhind guard the entrance to the Ehret mausoleum by Schickel & Ditmars in Pine plot. Photograph by Lee Sandstead.

Herbert Adams entitled *Guardian of the Tomb* was installed in 1932; it depicts an androgynous figure holding an ankh, an ancient Egyptian symbol representing eternal life. The mausoleum had been created by architect Robert Caterson after the death of Huntington's wife Elizabeth in 1888; Collis Huntington died in 1900. A bas-relief panel of Huntington by sculptor Bela Lyon Pratt can be found in the interior, one of several versions of the same portrait in profile.

Other forms of decorative metalwork are found in the cemetery in later decades. Master blacksmith Samuel Yellin contributed his art to the Harkness mausoleum in 1927 and the James Norman Hill mausoleum in 1930, for example. Marie Zimmerman designed the elaborate bronze doors for the Rudolph Metz columbarium in 1934.

Modernist Memorials

The 1920s began a period of experimentation in American sculpture, when many fine artists lost faith in Beaux-Arts ideals and naturalistic styles and became interested in working with a greater variety of materials than the marble and bronze that had dominated the academic sculptural tradition.[30] Modernist experimentation, based on European developments such as Cubism, Futurism, and Dada, was slower to appear in the essentially conservative cemetery than in art galleries. Traditional materials persisted at Woodlawn and other cemeteries due to the need for durability of monuments. But the 1920s represents one of the highpoints for artistic sculptural memorials at Woodlawn. A simplified symbolic mode, still based on figurative personifications, was often adopted with roots in Art Deco or a more geometrical Classical Revival, such as the Greek sources plumbed by Paul Manship in rendering the human form in new, less naturalistic ways. A more streamlined form emerged. There was also a return to carved stone amid the general new interest in varying materials and process.

Artist Onorio Ruotolo, for example, contributed his *The Idyll of Death* relief for the Luigi and Conchetta Fusco memorial in 1927 (Fig. 116). Moving toward a more abstract form carved in stone, his memorial seeks to deliver an idea of sorrowful parting rather than to create the illusion of a real scene the eye could see. According to one description, a dying virgin, at right, entrusts the lily of her purity to her guardian angel who sorrowfully takes it gently and reverently between his hands.[31] It is a poetic theme of tragic mysticism that resonates with such predecessors as Elihu Vedder's

Fig. 116. *The Idyll of Death* by Onorio Ruotolo is the monument to the Fusco family in Brookside plot. Photograph by Gavin Ashworth.

illustrations for Kahlil Gibran or the work of British pre-Raphaelite poets and artists such as Dante Gabriel Rossetti. But Ruotolo adopts simple patterns for the angel's wings and hair and an economy of line and shape for the figure's bodies to deliver his message of gentle yet deep emotion at death's arrival. The virgin looks away, her hands releasing the symbolic lily. The band in her hand bears the Fusco name, also emblazoned above. At the top of the stele is IHS, a monogram for the name of Jesus Christ, and below one sees a classical swag. The angel's figure is framed by a rough-cut background that articulates its contours and contributes to an "all-over" design, associated with the Art Deco style, which distributes the interest across the entire surface of the memorial. As a shallow pictorial relief, it is intended to be viewed only from the front by a viewer standing near the individual grave markers. No explicit explanation of the theme is provided. Ruotolo, who came to the United States from his native Naples at age 19, had made busts of such figures as Lenin, Enrico Caruso, Dante, Helen Keller, Abraham Lincoln, and Thomas Edison (titled *The Brother of Prometheus*) in his career. His work was promoted in New York's Italian language newspapers. He was a co-founder, with Attilio Piccirilli, of the Leonardo da Vinci Art School, which opened in 1923 on New York's Lower East Side. Ruotolo also designed the small 1931 relief at Woodlawn for the Frank Battaglia memorial, which shows a figure with a lamp greeting the sun.

Even more unusual in the cemetery is Ettore Cadorin's nude figures of Death and Resurrection, designed for the Miran and Zabelle Karagheusian memorial in 1921 (Fig. 117). Cast in bronze, the figures appear to be awakening or rising from beneath a heavy draped cloth. Miran Karagheusian was a rug manufacturer. Cadorin hoped to initiate a new movement in expressive memorial art. Nudity had long been associated with the universal in artistic tradition, not tying figures to

the costume of a particular time and place but making them fluid stand-ins for a larger idea or concept. Cadorin, born and educated in Venice, arrived in the United States in 1915, working in his early years in New York and then, after 1925, in California. He made monuments for cemeteries in Santa Barbara, Paris, Budapest, Bucharest, Holland and Australia as well as Woodlawn.[32] According to an article in *Art and Archaeology* at the time of this memorial's installation, "The artist aims with this work to give a new character to the sculpture of cemeteries less conventional, and with a deeper and more symbolic meaning."[33] His figures of Death and Resurrection are simplified, elongated forms suggesting the torpor of a sleep-like death and a rapture of awakening to a new life. Parts of the bodies remain enveloped in the block, and their long hair also becomes one with the bronze as it flows downward. "The

Fig. 117. *Death and Resurrection* by Ettore Cadorin for the Karagheusian memorial in Lakeview plot. Photograph by Lee Sandstead.

group represents the symbol of the Christian belief, according to which death is considered a passage from this life to the Eternal Life, through the resurrection of the spirit," the *Art and Archaeology* account states.[34] Perhaps this explains why cemetery managers accepted this unusual nudity and experimental style within Woodlawn – Christian iconography articulated in this case with modernist innovation.

Another more discreet example of expressive nudity was Sally James Farnham's well-known *At the End of the Day* for the grave of Vernon Castle (Fig. 118). It was erected at Woodlawn in 1922 by his widow and dancing partner, Irene Castle. The figure is a woman, with head and arms wearily drooping downward. Again, the nudity is intended to represent a universal figure, here exhausted by physical effort – as at the end of a dance routine – or spent by emotion, not the specific figure of the wife left behind, but all of humanity in this circumstance.[35] The sculpture sits in the center of a four-column exedra, once covered with vines, on a rough-hewn podium inscribed with an epitaph to Vernon, who died in 1918 during World War I "in the service of his country."

Fig. 118. *At the End of the Day* by Sally James Farnham is the monument to Vernon Castle in Park View plot. Avery Library, Drawings & Archives, Woodlawn Cemetery Records.

Irene Castle had at some point seen a plaster version that Farnham had first exhibited at the National Academy of Design in 1915; in 1922 she asked her to enlarge it for her husband's grave.[36] She initially referred to it as *Grief*; the modern title *At the End of the Day* was apparently only adopted later. The cemetery required lot owners to submit designs for such sculpture, and after Mrs. Castle informed the cemetery of her desire to have Farnham's piece erected in the cemetery, the sculptor sent photos to the cemetery office for review and also offered to show the Woodlawn managers a small model of the figure if they preferred to visit her studio.[37] Little is known of any cases where the cemetery officials might have tried to block any design found to be distasteful, but it is clear that they demanded to see drawings, photos, or models in advance during this period to ensure that they were in good taste. A photograph of a small-scale model of a semi-nude figure for the Margherita Mori monument (1927) by Charles Keck, for example, was submitted to the cemetery managers in advance and evidently found acceptable (Fig. 119). It represents a topless female figure, seated on a low, thick headstone, designed by Raymond Hood.

Farnham, a New York state native who was largely self-taught, made war memorials, busts, and decorative work during her career. She also designed the Orto memorial (1922), a stone relief of a woman compressed into a circular shape, and the Emma Biardot memorial (1921), a meditative seated figure in shallow relief, for Woodlawn. She was one of a handful of women sculptors who contributed pieces at Woodlawn, including Janet Scudder, Margaret French Cresson (the daughter of Daniel Chester French), Anna Hyatt Huntington, and Gertrude Vanderbilt Whitney.

Whitney designed the bronze figures and doors for a mysterious vertical shrine at one corner of

Fig. 119. The Margherita Mori monument in Clover plot was a collaboration between sculptor Charles Keck and architect Raymond Hood. Avery Library, Drawings & Archives, Woodlawn Cemetery Records.

the 22,000-square foot lot that memorializes the family of lawyer Samuel Untermyer. A contract made directly between the sculptress and patron in 1925 promised her $65,000 for the project upon completion, after acceptance of several stages of models.[38](Fig. 120)

The shrine is open on three sides with elaborate bronze doors decorated on the exterior with figures that appear to depict the stages of a woman's life – from youthful courtship to child-bearing and watchful remembrance. Floral symbols are found on the interior of the doors. Each door is also marked with a Greek word, roughly translated as Friendship and Comradery, Inspiration and Nurturing, Compassion and "She Who Gives Birth." The whole is raised on a nearly five-foot-high base so that the viewer must look up at the doors and darkened interior. Fluted square columns with garlands at their top mark each of the four corners of the tower and support the steeply stepped, ornate bronze roof. At the far end, steps lead down an embankment into the woods from the plot.

Inside the shrine, one sees a woman with arms outstretched ascending to the afterlife against the backdrop of the closed wall. A gaunt cloaked male figure kneels in front of her and reaches out with one hand. A standing female turns and faces the front door of the shrine. All of the figures are barefoot, simplified, and elongated, life-size or slightly larger. No public explanation was ever offered as to the iconography, which blueprints show replaced an original concept for a more traditional memorial at that location.[39] What share of the puzzling design was Whitney's idea or Untermyer's is unknown.

Fig. 120. Bronze doors and interior sculptural figures within by Gertrude Vanderbilt Whitney are part of the Untermyer memorial in Cliff plot, designed by Paul Chalfin as a complex ensemble of architecture, sculpture, and garden design. Avery Library, Drawings & Archives, Woodlawn Cemetery Records.

Fig. 121. The Bliss monument by sculptor Robert Aitken and architect William Welles Bosworth commands the hillside of Walnut plot. Avery Library, Drawings & Archives, Woodlawn Cemetery Records.

Fig. 122. Paul Manship's original bronze sculpture for the Marshall monument in Sassafras plot was later replaced by the same form carved in marble. Avery Library, Drawings & Archives, Presbrey-Leland collection.

Whitney, the eldest daughter of Cornelius Vanderbilt II and wife of millionaire sportsman Henry Payne Whitney, was an arts patron as well as sculptor and writer. She studied sculpture in New York and Paris, and her privileged status helped her build a significant career, as the *New York Times* once put it, as a "Poor Little Rich Girl."[40] Her memorial commissions included the Titanic Memorial in Washington. She had been a longtime acquaintance of Paul Chalfin, whom Untermyer retained for his Woodlawn memorial, of which the shrine was only one element. Untermyer, whose wife Minnie had died in 1924, was a prominent corporate lawyer and then trust-buster and an ally of Woodrow Wilson who worked for legal reforms. He also worked on behalf of Jewish rights in his career and, as a philanthropist, headed the Palestine Foundation fund for several years. He had a great personal interest in landscaping, having commissioned William Welles Bosworth to design the Persian- and Greek-themed gardens at Grey Walls, his estate in Yonkers. The landscaping of the U-shaped memorial plot in Woodlawn was carefully designed with a sundial set in a Star of David patterned plaza.

While most cemetery memorials were highly private commissions employing sculptors selected personally by survivors or by estates, one female patron, Anna Blakesley Bliss,[41] went to the unusual step of holding a "secret" competition for her unusual 1917 monument (Fig. 121).

A year after the accidental death of her stepdaughter, Cora Barnes, who fell from a fourth floor of her residence, Mrs. Bliss commissioned architect William Welles Bosworth to organize a competition for a memorial. Bosworth wrote to the cemetery asking for photographs of the site to guide candidates' submissions, advising a Woodlawn official on June 13, 1912, "I believe you understand the great importance which Mrs. Bliss attaches to having this matter kept entirely secret for various reasons. I trust that you will have her wishes observed most strictly. The competition for the models is being held anonymously and the client's name does not appear at all in this connection."[42]

Nearly four years later, *American Art News* reported that artist Robert Aitken had nearly completed his winning design, having received the commission after "a competition of six well known sculptors." The article also described the group, saying, "The two figures which it embraces are of heroic size and are symbolical

Fig. 123. The bronze and black granite Romney memorial by Alexander Archipenko is located in Golden Rod plot. Photograph by Lee Sandstead.

of the soul leaving the body, the idea being that of Mrs. Bliss. The figures are of Faith and Hope."[43]

The spirit-forms of a man and woman, carved by the Piccirilli Brothers from Aitken's model, stand atop a low curving bench, with spiral forms at each end, suggestive of flowing water. Chiseled on the bench is the quotation, "Our souls have sight of that immortal sea which brought us hither," which comes from William Wordsworth's ode, "Imitations of Immortality from Recollections of Early Childhood." In the poem, the lines suggest that our souls can reconnect with the formless, timeless realm from which we arrived as infants, when we were closer to the celestial before engaging the material world. A bronze plate opens into a cinerarium in the back of the monument where the ashes of Barnes and Mrs. Bliss were placed. The monument was named one of the best of the year in the January 1918 *Monumental News*, which declared, "The whole scheme of the monument is highly individual and the result of the conception of the clients and the architect and sculptor."[44]

Experimentation continued at Woodlawn over the decades. Garden sculptures, sundials, and smaller decorative commissions often provided work for artists in cemeteries in this period. This reflected general trends in American sculpture, which became more for the museum and private collector, with interest shifting to smaller sculpture for the interior rather than grand scale public monuments for City Beautiful exteriors and outdoor space. In 1946-1947, the artist Paul Manship contributed a delicate form he had been exploring, two hands emerging from a cloud and holding a star, for the Marshall monument at Woodlawn. Manship is famous for his Art Deco works, which combine semi-naturalistic shapes with stylized patterns as in his 1930s statue of *Prometheus* at New York's Rockefeller Center. The small memorial at Woodlawn, placed atop a slender column, memorializes Lane Robertson Yarborough Marshall, who died in a car accident (Fig. 122). Her mother, artist and writer Lucille Robertson Marshall, arranged with Manship to use his model, which seems related to other explorations by the sculptor of the cycle of life, the celestial sphere and stars. It was executed with his approval by the Presbrey-Leland Monument Company.[45]

A modernist reinterpretation of a funerary urn was the work of Ukrainian-born sculptor Alexander Archipenko. The artist, who played with different shapes and materials of varied colors and qualities, had explored Cubism and Futurism during his career. Here the urn, fashioned in bronze in 1946, is composed in nearly abstract curved forms and rests atop four geometrically precise legs of a pedestal carved in Russian Black granite (Fig. 123). Archipenko worked in Paris and New York. This seven-foot-high sculpture was designed as the memorial of the family of Alfred Romney, an art collector. The detailed drawings Archipenko sent to the cemetery for approval of the monument design are in the Woodlawn archive at Avery Library. Archipenko used a revolutionary style to refer to an ancient form of an urn, here marking the spot where cremated remains of two family members were placed. Archipenko's wife, Angelica, in 1951, designed a sculpture of a seated and shrouded woman for the Archipenko family monument in another area of the cemetery. The bronze sculpture was titled *Premonition Self Portrait Created by Angelica*.

The sculptural landscape of Woodlawn has continued to evolve in the ensuing decades, with an array of styles, from traditional to experimental, overlapping in our own era. Monuments range from revivals of the earliest themes to highly personal new forms – a continuation of the eclecticism and innovation that has created a developing, ever distinctive space for memory.

1. *Annual Report of the Trustees of the Wood-Lawn Cemetery to the Lot-Owners for the Year 1867* (New York: Office of the Wood-Lawn Cemetery, 1868), 11. Prepared by R.E.K. Whiting, superintendent. See Woodlawn Cemetery Records, 1863-1999, Drawings & Archives, Avery Architectural & Fine Arts Library, Columbia University (hereafter cited as Woodlawn Cemetery Records).

2. Ibid.

3. The monument bears similarities to the memorial to Andrew Culver in Green-Wood Cemetery, New York, who died in 1871 and which was signed by Casoni and Isola, according to Jeff Richman, Green-Wood historian. There the central vertical element is a broken tree trunk. *See* https://www.green-wood.com/2011/master-carvers-casoni-isola/

4. *Annual Report*, 14.

5. Foundation Book Two, Woodlawn Cemetery Records.

6. An undated catalogue from the New England Granite Works listed nearly 150 tombs and mausoleums at Woodlawn as its productions. See http://quarriesandbeyond.org/

7. Palmer's design was carved by New England Granite, and it was repeated in a different stone for the Swift monument at Cedar Hill Cemetery in Hartford.

8. "Monuments," *American Art Review* 2, no. 11 (September 1881): 213. Plassmann also was the author of two books, *Modern Gothic Ornaments* (1875) and *Designs for Furniture* (1877); see James Goode, *Washington Sculpture* (Baltimore: Johns Hopkins University Press, 2008), 791.

9. See Pottier correspondence file, Woodlawn Cemetery Records.

10. "Pulitzer Memorial a Fine Exedra Type," *Monumental News* 28: 1 (January 1916): cover, 31.

11. "Porter Kills Two in Fifth Av. Shop," *New York Times*, July 24, 1918; "Governor Saves Slayer," *New York Times*, January 3, 1920.

12. Daniel Chester French to Mrs. Martiny, July 3, 1927, Martiny Papers, Archives of American Art, Washington D.C.

13. Martiny worked with Presbrey-Leland Monument Company, contractors, and architect William Henry Deacy (1889-1967) on the project, and the statue was cast by Roman Bronze Works, according to the description in *Monumental News* 33:1 (January 1921): 21.

14. *The Woodlawn Cemetery, New York* (New York: Woodlawn Cemetery, 1925).

15. "Herbert M Kinsley Dead," *New York Times*, September 23, 1894, http://query.nytimes.com/mem/archive-free/pdf?res=F60F11FD3A5515738DDDAA0A94D1405B485F0D3.

16. An apparent unapproved copy is the Thurman memorial, ca. 1916, in Atlanta's Oakland Cemetery, in pink marble by J.S. Novelli. See Josephine Murphy, *Novelli: A Forgotten Sculptor* (Boston: Brandon Books, 2003), 87, plate 56. At the same time, French's sculpture bears strange similarities to a figure in the Murchison monument, Wilmington, North Carolina, by James Sharkey, dated in the 1880s.

17. On the National Sculpture Society exhibition, see Charles De Kay, "National Sculpture Exhibition," *New York Times*, May 15, 1898, http://query.nytimes.com/mem/archive-free/pdf?res=FB0A15FD3C5C11738DDDAC0994DD40 5B8885F0D3.

18. Bruce Donaldson, "American Sculpture at Buffalo," *American Magazine of Art* 7:10 (August 1916): 417.

19. See Josef Vincent Lombardo, *Attilio Piccirilli: Life of an American Sculptor* (New York: Pitman Publishing Corporation, 1944), 196-198, 343, 345, and 391. On the Piccirillis, see also Adeline Adams, "A Family of Sculptors" in *American Magazine of Art* 12 (July 1921): 223-30.; and Mary Shelley and Bill Caroll, "The Piccirilli Studio," *Bronx County Historical Society Journal* 36 (spring 1999): 1-12.

20. Lombardo, *Attilio Piccirilli*, 197.

21. C. de Kay, "A Bronze Door by Bartlett" *New York Times*, November 7, 1897, http://query.nytimes.com/mem/archive-free/pdf?res=FA0913FB395811738DDDAE0894D9415B8785F0D3

22. The piece-mold process of casting predominated at that time. Michael Shapiro, *Bronze Casting and American Sculpture, 1850-1900* (Newark: University of Delaware Press, 1985), 128-32. Copper is the primary element of bronze, and Senator Clark was known as the "Copper King of Montana" as director of the United Verde Copper Company. According to Shapiro, Clark secretly acquired the Henry-Bonnard foundry before the turn of the century so that it could provide the bronze work he wished for in the new house he and his second wife planned on Fifth Avenue, and he provided the capital for its expansion. Thus, it seems possible that the work on the mausoleum door led Clark to influence the U.S. art bronze foundry industry.

23. On the relief, see Thayer Tolles, *Perspectives on American Sculpture before 1925: Metropolitan Museum of Art Symposia* (New York: Metropolitan Museum of Art, 2003), 89-91.

24. William A. Clark to Paul Wayland Bartlett, Dec. 7, 1896. Paul Wayland Bartlett Papers, Archives of American Art, Smithsonian Institution, Washington, D.C.

25. Arthur Hoeber, "Robert I. Aitken, A.N.A., an American Sculptor," *International Studio* 50, no. 197, July 1913: 3, 7. Aitken also designed the door of the Greenhut mausoleum at Woodlawn.

26. William Walton, "A Higher Quality in Funerary Monuments," *American Architect* 100, no. 1854, July 5, 1911. Weinman also contributed the relief for the Stewart mausoleum, 1914, at Woodlawn.

27. Josephine Murphy, *Novelli: A Forgotten Sculptor* (Boston: Branden Books, 2003), 78-79.

28. On Federici, see Flavia Alaya, et al., *Gaetano Federici, 1880-1946, the Artist as Historian* (Paterson: Passaic County Historical Society in cooperation with the Paterson Museum, 1980).

29. November 4, 1901 agreement between J. Massey Rhind and George (Geerg) Ehret. Ehret mausoleum major monument file, Woodlawn Cemetery Records.

30. Daniel Robbins, "Statues to Sculpture: From the Nineties to the Thirties," in *200 Years of American Sculpture* (New York: Whitney Museum of American Art, 1976), 137-38.

31. See Frances Winwar, *Ruotolo, Man and Artist* (New York: Liveright Publishing Company, 1949), 22.

32. *Contemporary American Sculpture* (New York: National Sculpture Society, 1929), 37.

33. "Current Notes and Comments: 'Death and Resurrection' by Ettore Cadorin," *Art and Archaeology: The Arts throughout the Ages* 11, no. 5 (May 1921): 221.

34. Ibid.

35. Irene Castle stated in her autobiography that "the rumor got around" that she had posed for Farnham's sculpture, adding, "It was not true, of course, although, beautiful as it was, I wished I could say I had." Irene Castle, *Castles in the Air* (Garden City, New York: Doubleday & Company, 1958), 183.

36. The original work for the cemetery was in marble, but it was replaced in the 1950s by a bronze version after the stone had become discolored and somewhat degraded by exposure.

37. See Irene Castle to Woodlawn Cemetery, Aug. 12, 1921, and Sally Farnham to cemetery officials, August 29, 1921, with photo by De Witt Ward. Castle major monument file, Woodlawn Cemetery Records.

38. Memorandum of Agreement, February 1925, between Gertrude Whitney and Samuel Untermyer, Archives of American Art, Smithsonian Institution, frame 1172-73, reel 2368.

39. See Untermyer major monument files, Woodlawn Cemetery Records.

40. "Poor Little Rich Girl and Her Art, Mrs. Harry Payne Whitney's Struggle to be Taken Seriously as a Sculptor Without Having Starved in a Garret," *New York Times*, November 9, 1917, http://query.nytimes.com/mem/archive-free/pdf?res=F40D13F73A5C1B728DDDA00894D9415B898DF1D3.

41. Anna Bliss, who died in 1935 at age 84, was a philanthropist with homes in California and New York; she had made gifts to the Metropolitan Museum of Art and the Town Hall of New York.

42. Letter from William Welles Bosworth to Woodlawn Cemetery, to the attention of Mr. Diering, June 13, 1912, Bliss major monuments file, Woodlawn Cemetery Records.

43. "Notes of Art and Artists," *American Art News*, 14:22, March 4, 1916: 5.

44. "Best Cemetery Monuments of the Year," *Monumental News*, 30, no. 1 (January 1918): 18-20.

45. Correspondence is found in the Avery Library as well as the Margaret Cassidy and John Paul Manship Collection in Gloucester, Massachusetts. My thanks to curator Rebecca Reynolds and archivist Sharon Spieldenner of the Manship collection for their assistance.

BEHIND CLOSED DOORS:
NOTABLE STAINED GLASS WINDOWS AT WOODLAWN CEMETERY

ALICE COONEY FRELINGHUYSEN

Stained glass windows, long associated with the embellishment of church interiors, became in late nineteenth-century America an integral part of the decorative scheme of mausoleums. Nowhere is this more evident than at Woodlawn Cemetery where the best artists of the period, both foreign and domestic, were commissioned to design memorial windows for the upper echelons of New York society. While there has been a recent surge in interest in ecclesiastical stained glass windows,[1] the study of those windows designed for mausoleums is relatively overlooked. The fact is thoroughly understandable considering that mausoleums, by their very nature, are private, and often such windows appear behind heavy bronze doors making them inaccessible to all but family members of the deceased. The other more regrettable reason is that many of the windows have been vandalized and even stolen from such mausoleums. In spite of the lack of documentation, however, mausoleum stained glass forms a significant aspect of memorial art during the late nineteenth and twentieth centuries, correlating to that designed for churches during the comparable period. As such, the glass at Woodlawn provides a virtual compendium of stained glass styles and techniques over a nearly fifty-year period, from the late 1870s to the late 1920s.

The subjects represented in the stained glass windows at Woodlawn Cemetery are remarkably varied. Predictably, those associated with Christ's Resurrection predominate. For instance, the Ascension, in both the Amsinck and Martin mausoleums, is rendered in completely different techniques – one in opalescent glass and the other in the more traditional painted and stained glass – but their compositions are nearly identical, suggesting the popularity of this theme (see Figs. 127, 128). Other subjects like Christ on the Way to Emmaus on the Day of Resurrection, or Christ in Majesty, were considered appropriately symbolic of sending a loved one to heaven. Makers might also have introduced a subtle yet specific reference to the deceased. In the case of the John La Farge window in the Lamont mausoleum, for example, the angel of grief is depicted as a young woman, referencing the tender age of Lamont's deceased daughter in whose memory the mausoleum was commissioned. La Farge was known to have also personalized certain windows with painted visages as portraits, which may be the case here. New subjects, such as bucolic landscapes, were introduced at the turn of the century, primarily by Tiffany Studios. One favorite subject, seen on a

PLATE 4. Door opened to the interior of the Belmont mausoleum in Whitewood plot. Photograph by Gavin Ashworth.

BEHIND CLOSED DOORS   121

Fig. 124. Magnolias and Irises, window, from Frank family mausoleum, Salem Fields Cemetery, New York. Tiffany Studios, New York, ca. 1908. 60 x 42 in. (153 x 106.7 cm). The Metropolitan Museum of Art, Anonymous Gift, in memory of Mr. and Mrs. A. B. Frank, 1981 (1981.159). Image © The Metropolitan Museum of Art.

window for the Frank mausoleum in the Salem Fields Cemetery, Brooklyn, and now at The Metropolitan Museum of Art, was a landscape with a river meandering through a mountain valley (Fig. 124), considered emblematic of the River of Life of the deceased and interpreted in numerous variations. Likewise, as seen in the Westinghouse mausoleum at Woodlawn (Fig. 125), the selection of flowers, such as the white Resurrection lily, might suggest the theme.

Imported Windows

American studios provided most of the stained glass windows at Woodlawn Cemetery. Only a handful of foreign makers are represented, and then mainly by firms that ultimately maintained offices in New York City as well as in their home country. Two such examples are the Franz Mayer Studio from Munich and the firm of Heaton, Butler and Bayne of London.

The mausoleum built for Eccles Gillender (1810-1877), one of the earliest at Woodlawn, also houses one of the earliest stained glass windows at the cemetery (Fig. 126). Gillender was a highly successful tobacco merchant whose fortune was made during and following the Civil War. Two years after his death in 1877, his wife, Augusta Lovett Gillender, purchased a lot at Woodlawn on which to build the mausoleum to house the remains of her husband. Although the structure appears modest when compared with the scale and flamboyance of many later mausoleums at Woodlawn, it is important to remember that in 1877, it must have seemed grand indeed. Augusta was well off in her own right, as the daughter of successful building contractor and mortgage banker George Lovett.[2]

The early date of the Gillender mausoleum predates the heyday of the opalescent glass studios of Louis C. Tiffany and John La Farge for ecclesiastic work who were both just beginning their careers in stained glass. Although there were domestic stained glass studios in operation in New York City and other cities during the late 1870s, it was more common at this date to employ foreign makers, such as the thriving Mayer Studio from Munich, which had a serious foothold in America. The Mayer firm was founded in Munich in 1847-48 by Josef Gabriel Mayer for the production of all manner of ecclesiastical furnishings. In their early days they subcontracted their work on stained glass windows to independent Munich artists, but by 1865 they had established their own stained glass department, under the direction of Franz Xaver Zettler (1841-1916), Mayer's son-in-law. Zettler's tenure at Mayer was relatively short-lived, and he founded his own firm in 1870 (although his firm re-joined Mayer in 1939). The Mayer firm operated for a number of generations, and is still in business today. For their ecclesiastic work in North America, they were known primarily for their Catholic commissions.[3] Their growth in this business eventually prompted them to open a New York City branch office in 1888 which employed numerous artists at 124 West 23rd Street.

The vast majority of their windows in America are in the Munich pictorial style, which may be seen in the window for the Gillender mausoleum. The archangel St. Michael, clad in armor, is portrayed holding his attributes of a sword and shield with a slayed dragon at his feet, one foot holding him down. In religious iconography, he is considered the warrior and judge who defeated Satan, represented by the dragon. Considered the protector of soldiers and Christians in general, Michael was also thought of as the angel of death, carrying the souls of all the deceased to heaven, and hence a fitting subject for a mauso-

Fig. 125. Possibly Tiffany Studios, Landscape window with lilies for West-inghouse mausoleum in Whitewood plot. Photograph by Gavin Ashworth.

leum. While Raphael's famous painting of St. Michael portrays him in a more active, dynamic pose in the process of slaying the serpent – well known and also translated into stained glass by Tiffany Studios on more than one occasion[4] – the Mayer depiction is a more static, yet triumphant pose. The figure is well articulated with jewel-like colors in a robe of rich ruby glass adorned in gold with luminous blue wings, while the slain serpent is in a vivid green. The figure fills the window and is framed in an elegant architectural framework, which complements the Gothic style of the granite structure. Florence Delaplaine Beekman Amsinck commissioned the English firm of Heaton, Butler and Bayne to supply the window for the mausoleum she erected in memory of her husband Gustav Amsinck (1837-1909) (Fig. 127). It was only fitting that she provide a grand resting place for her second husband, who upon his death, left the lion's share of his estate to her, including all of his property in New York and in Hamburg, plus one million dollars outright and the income from a million dollar trust fund. (In 1912, she was married for the third time, to New York statesman Hamilton Fish.)

Fig. 126. Franz Mayer, Munich, Archangel Michael and the dragon window for Gillender mausoleum in Ravine plot, ca. 1879. Photograph by Gavin Ashworth.

The firm she commissioned to execute the window that graced the mausoleum for her husband was established in 1852 as a partnership of Clement Heaton (1824-1882), and James Butler (1830-1913). For the most part they operated their workshop and showroom at 14 Garrick Street, Covent Garden, in London. Heaton, who had worked for the prestigious stained glass firm of William Holland, made a lasting contribution through the development of new pigments of glass paints and considerably expanded the options in that line. Butler was an experienced glazier. Robert T. Bayne (1837-1915), who became the firm's chief designer after working for the other successful British pre-Raphaelite stained glass enterprise of Clayton and Bell, joined as a partner in 1862. Surviving drawings that descended in Bayne's family attest to the precision and detail in the firm's stained glass proposals, as well as a firm grasp of ecclesiastic subject matter.

Heaton, Butler and Bayne provided windows worldwide, executing commissions from Australia and New Zealand to India, Africa, and Japan. Their strongest presence was in the United States, however, and especially in New York City where they maintained an office at 437 Fifth Avenue. The window for the Amsinck mausoleum was appropriately a depiction of Christ in Ascension, flanked by two angels and ascending into the clouds with rays streaming down, and diminutive buildings and mountains receding far below. The palette is distinctive in its predominance of blues and purples offset by Christ in brilliant red robes. Reflective of tenets of the Aesthetic movement, the hues are tertiary, grayed ones, forsaking all primary colors except for Christ's red robes. The window bears an inscription with the comforting words, "Fear Thou Not for I am with Thee, be not dismayed for I am thy God" [Isaiah 41:10], in Gothic script at the bottom of the window. By way of comparison, the Heaton, Butler and Bayne Ascension is the nearly identical composition executed at virtually the same time by Duffner and Kimberly for the John Martin mausoleum, which employed opalescent glass (Fig. 128), rather than the traditional "antique" stained and painted glass. Relatively monochromatic, Christ and the angels are all in white robes, with textured and folded glass suggesting the drapery folds. Rigidly symmetrical in composition, the window is suffused with soft tonalities seen in the angels' lavender wings and pastel shades throughout. The exceptions are the golden halos which add a bright richness in contrast to the cool overall tonalities.

Heaton, Butler and Bayne were competitive with domestic and foreign makers in the United States market. Their American presence was facilitated by their relationship with the Gorham Manufacturing Company in Providence, Rhode Island, which contracted with the English firm in 1886

Fig. 127. Heaton, Butler and Bayne, London, Ascension window for Amsinck mausoleum in Observatory plot, ca. 1909. Photograph by Gavin Ashworth.

Fig. 128. Duffner and Kimberly, *Resurrection* window. John Martin Mausoleum in Pine plot, c. 1908. Photograph by Gavin Ashworth.

to be their American agents. They continued to represent the Heaton firm until about 1904, when Gorham established its own stained glass production. Thus, the Amsinck window dates to the period when the firm established their own representatives in New York.

Both Mayer and Heaton, Butler and Bayne were firms that practiced the traditional techniques of stained glass – utilizing white and colored glass, and employing specialized glass painters to work with enamels and opaque vitreous paint that would be fired to achieve a degree of permanence – to produce the pictorial details and modeling. Highlights in gold were achieved by silver stain, the application of silver nitrate on the reverse of the pane, which when fired turned a rich golden color that varied from lemon yellow to almost bronze. This traditional method was practiced by both European and American artists.

American Windows

Although D. Maitland Armstrong (1836-1918) is perhaps best known today for his work in opalescent glass as a contemporary of John La Farge and Louis C. Tiffany, with whom he worked briefly, he was also a proponent of the more traditional glass staining techniques that were nearly ubiquitous abroad and that aligned with traditional revivals of the Gothic style in architecture. Armstrong set up a stained glass studio at Washington Square in the 1890s, and worked closely with his daughter, Helen Maitland Armstrong (1869-1948), who drew many of the watercolor and ink designs and car-

Fig. 129. Helen Maitland Armstrong, Angel Gabriel Window for Belmont mausoleum in Whitewood plot, c. 1910. Stained glass. Photograph by Gavin Ashworth.

toons for windows as well as executed the actual painting on glass. She was considered especially talented in her painting of faces and hands.[5] Armstrong's neo-Gothic style was perfectly suited to the elaborate architecture of the mortuary chapel designed by the architects Hunt & Hunt for Alva Erskine Belmont (1853-1933). Mrs. Belmont, one of the most notorious women of New York and Newport society, previously divorced William Kissam Vanderbilt in an era when such actions were deemed shocking, and then shortly thereafter married perhaps the equally rich Oliver Hazard Perry Belmont (1858-1908). When Belmont died suddenly in 1908, just twelve years after their marriage, Alva set out to construct one of Woodlawn Cemetery's most extravagant structures to memorialize her husband. Designed in a flamboyant Gothic architectural style by the firm of Hunt & Hunt (the successor firm to Richard Morris Hunt), the building emulated the Chapel of Saint Hubert at the Chateaux d'Amboise in France, reduced to a much smaller scale. The mausoleum was adorned with a total of nine windows, with five narrow lancet windows in the apse, two decorative windows of geometric white glass with motifs in shield-shaped reserves and Gothic tracery flanking three central figural windows, all in a neo-Gothic style complementary to the architecture of the building. The three figural windows that dominate the apse depict three archangels: St. Michael on the left, St. Raphael on the right, and the center with St. Gabriel in an elegant medieval pose (Fig. 129). The central panel also bears Helen Maitland Armstrong's name.

As depicted by Armstrong, Gabriel, as the Messenger of God and Angel of the Annunciation, wears resplendent robes of blue, gold, and ermine; bears both attributes of lilies and the scepter; and carries a scroll inscribed "Ave Marie, Gratia Plena" (Hail Mary, Full of Grace). The lavishness of the depiction of Gabriel is consistent with the ostentation of the Belmont mausoleum itself and with Alva Belmont's extravagance. This window, in a rigid fourteenth-century style, contrasts dramatically with another depiction of Gabriel by Armstrong. In a sensitive watercolor and ink design drawing she made of the subject for another stained glass window, the artist has rejected the stringent medieval mode with its stiff figure, overwhelming architecture, and limited color palette in favor of an angel depicted in a softer naturalistic rendering, more aligned with the work of the Pre-Raphaelite painters (Fig. 130). The figure, now without crown, scepter, and ermine, simply carries but one stem of white lilies.

The stained glass in the Belmont chapel complemented other artistic Gothic-style ornament in the chapel such as an elaborate carved frieze tympanum depicting St. Hubert's vision of Christ in the antlers of a stag by François Tonetti (1864-1920), suggesting the architectural source for the mausoleum, and a mural by William Mackay (1876-1939). So pleased was Alva Belmont with Armstrong's work in stained glass that when she planned a large Hunt & Hunt designed addition to the house (on Madison Avenue and 51st Street in New York) she and her husband were building at the time of his death, she commissioned Armstrong to make a series of Gothic-style windows of medieval subjects.

A window Helen Armstrong designed a little over a decade later for the Harkness mausoleum reveals her delicate artistry, yet in an entirely different mode (Fig. 131). The building of the mausoleum was undertaken by William L. Harkness (1856-1919), philanthropist and heir to a fortune based on inherited shares of Standard Oil Company. Although the plot was purchased by Harkness in 1914 and the plans for it were approved by him in 1919, the mausoleum was not completed until 1921, two years after his death, through the auspices of the Harkness estate.[6] (His widow, Edith H. Harkness (1865-1947), ordered the addition of a terrace and a sundial in 1923.[7]) Hunt & Hunt, the same architects as the Belmont mausoleum, designed the stark mausoleum in imitation of a Greek Doric peripteral temple with twenty-eight fluted Doric columns. Perhaps the architects suggested Armstrong to provide the stained glass window, given that they had earlier used her windows for both the Belmont memorial chapel at Woodlawn and the Belmonts' New York City house.

The Harkness window is roughly square in shape, and features an angel at one side, kneeling with a scroll and the popular funerary inscription, "O Lord support us all the daylong of this troubled life until the shadows lengthen and the evening comes and the busy world is over and our work is done. Then of thy great mercy grant us a safe lodging and a holy rest and peace at last."[8] The style of the window, simply painted on white glass, is a departure from the more colorful and more fully leaded stained glass windows. Predominantly in grisaille tones, it presents a trompe l'oeil depiction of a stone relief effectively portrayed as if the panel was carved with stone floral rosettes in each corner, and the angel chiseled in relief from the background. The exceptions are the head and arms which are painted with enamels to suggest flesh tones, blue eyes, blond hair and an ivy crown. The painting style brings to mind the delicacy of the heads of much smaller scale in her window design renderings such as that of St. Gabriel (see Fig. 131). Likewise, the composition and delineation of the angel and wings are reminiscent of Armstrong's work as a book illustrator, which features

Fig. 130. Helen Maitland Armstrong, St. Gabriel: Design for Stained Glass Window, 1890-1918." Watercolor and pen and ink, 12 15/16 x 3 1/2 in. The Metropolitan Museum of Art, Gift of Helen Bienstock, Cynthia MacKay Keegan and Frank E. Johnson, 2012 (2012.400.5). Image © The Metropolitan Museum of Art.

· G · A · B · R · I · E · L ·

Fig. 131. Helen Maitland Armstrong, Angel. William Harkness mausoleum in Golden Rod plot, 1921. Stained glass. Signed: Helen Maitland Armstrong, 1921. Photograph by Gavin Ashworth.

Fig. 132. Helen Maitland Armstrong illustration. *Ad Astra: Being Selections from the Divine Comedy of Dante* (New York: R.H. Russell, 1902), binding and decorations by Margaret Armstrong; illustrations by Helen Maitland Armstrong [Metropolitan Museum of Art, acc. No. 2012.128.8]. The Metropolitan Museum of Art. Image © The Metropolitan Museum of Art.

similar religious figures and epitaphs (Fig. 132).[9] The minimal palette accentuates its affinities to black-and-white book illustration. Its grisaille tonalities and its subtle pastel tones also evoke the creamy tones of opalescent windows then also in vogue, and which were also part of the repertoire of the Maitland Armstrong studios.

Opalescent Windows

Daniel S. Lamont (1851-1905), the former private secretary to President Grover Cleveland and United States Secretary of War, selected John La Farge (1835-1910), the noted stained-glass artist and proponent of the opalescent style of windows very much in fashion, to design and fabricate the window that would grace the mausoleum he built at Woodlawn to memorialize his daughter (Fig. 133).[10] Julia Lamont (1883-1902) died tragically at the young age of nineteen of a stroke while summering at their cottage in Sorrento, a town across Frenchman's Bay from Bar Harbor, Maine.[11] La Farge chose as his subject the allegory of Grief, all too appropriate for her inconsolable family. The subject is suggested in this context by a young woman, who may have born a resemblance to the deceased Julia. Her eyes are downcast and her hands fall slightly extended to her sides. Rose blossoms and blue cornflowers appear to drop from her hands and fall to the ground below, and suggest the transitory nature of life. As is typical of La Farge's work during this period, the woman is draped in classical garb. Again characteristic of La Farge is the elaborate frame, made to simulate an egg-and-dart and Greek key architectural molding in leaded glass in jewel tones of blue and gold.

John La Farge, along with Louis Comfort Tiffany, revolutionized the look of stained glass in America with the development of opalescent glass. This glass's characteristics utilized the coloration, depth, and texture in the glass itself for pictorial effect, along with innovations in leading the individual glass pieces together. Rendering the three-dimensional form in glass without the use of glass paint was a challenge faced by both Tiffany and La Farge. While Tiffany would develop a method of manipulating the glass to achieve modeling and especially the forms and folds of drapery, La Farge took a different path. His method involved fusing together with copper wire long, skinny, individual pieces of glass in different shades of the same hue to achieve a similar effect. As he described the technique: "The use of glass, fused together in patterns without leads ... is a sort of variation of cloisonné made through joining glass by thin filaments of metal fused to the glass."[12] The Lamont window is an especially fine example of this new technique which renders the classical drapery of the figure in rich jewel toned amethyst and gold glass.

The window is signed by both La Farge and Thomas Wright (1856-1918), and dated 1904. Wright, along with John Calvin, was La Farge's main assistant and chief glazier. The two men began work for him as early as 1881, shortly after he embarked on stained glass work, and remained with him

through the end of his career. This window is relatively unusual in that it bears both La Farge's and Wright's signatures. The Lamont window relates to *Spring*, completed two years before for William C. Whitney's Long Island house, now in the collection of the Philadelphia Museum of Art. Its similarities are especially evident in the winged figure, the closely related drapery, and the blossoms floating downward against the brilliant blue background to the blossoms below. Indeed, Lamont's business connections with Whitney may have played a role in commissioning La Farge to memorialize his daughter in leaded glass.[13]

Although Tiffany executed numerous windows at Woodlawn, La Farge executed only two. Much earlier in 1886 he provided the glass jewel encrusted decorative windows for the mausoleum of George L. Lorillard (1843-1892), who was related to La Farge by marriage.[14] He also planned the mosaic decoration for the William A. Clark mausoleum, but his suggestions were never executed.[15] Ultimately, La Farge was so taken with Woodlawn Cemetery that he wished to have a mausoleum built for himself there after his death. Unfortunately, he was seriously in debt at the time of his death, and his wife Margaret was forced to make the most difficult decision of not honoring the specific in-

Fig. 133. John La Farge and Thomas Wright, New York, Angel of Grief window for Lamont mausoleum in Walnut plot, ca. 1903. Photograph by Gavin Ashworth.

structions in her husband's will. With the estate in debt in the amount of $35,000, she was unable to afford the $3,000 required to purchase a plot at Woodlawn and erect a mausoleum, and instead, moved his body, already in a temporary crypt at Woodlawn, to the family mausoleum at Green-Wood Cemetery.[16]

Like La Farge, Louis Comfort Tiffany (1848-1933) was an innovator in stained glass, utilizing the new opalescent glass. The stained glass studios he founded produced windows for cemeteries throughout the United States. He introduced a color range wider than any hitherto imagined in the medium, as well as textured, mottled, and confetti glass, all of which helped to convey pictorial elements solely in glass without the use of traditional vitreous paint. This revolutionary technique swept the country and became de rigueur for churches being built during the late nineteenth and early twentieth centuries. Opalescent windows were so popular, and thought to have been so prestigious, that many churches replaced earlier stained glass windows with opalescent windows. The ascent of Tiffany's career coincided closely with the growth of the park cemetery movement, which roughly dates to the decades following the Civil War into the first decades of the twentieth century, and the desire by successful and wealthy families to memorialize their loved ones with grand stone mausoleums. Stained glass provided further embellishment for these private temples for the dead.

Nearly forty windows documented to Louis Comfort Tiffany and Tiffany Studios alone grace the interiors of mausoleums at Woodlawn, all designed as private memorial commissions. No other studio comes close to the number produced by that prestigious New York firm. Indeed, the selection at Woodlawn presents a veritable microcosm of Tiffany's career from at least the late 1880s through the late 1920s. Tiffany presented his firm as the premier studio for the mausoleums then being built in the country. Beginning with his first incorporated firm, The Tiffany Glass Company, memorial windows were included as part of their scope of work, although they did not mention mausoleums specifically.[17]

In addition to windows, however, Tiffany Studios set themselves up as a full-service provider for ecclesiastic decorations of all kinds, establishing in 1889 a separate Ecclesiastical Department that handled this division of their work. Their promotional pamphlet *Memorials in Glass and Stone* provided a comprehensive listing: "Figure windows, mosaic windows, medallion windows, landscape windows, glass mosaic tablets, marble and mosaic tablets, marble and bronze tablets, cast bronze tablets, figure mosaics, decorative mosaics, ornamental mosaics, architectural mosaics … mausoleums, tablet monuments, Celtic crosses, table monuments, ledger stones, sarcophagi, headstones, cinerary urns."[18]

In that and other publications, most of the memorial windows were designated for churches. However, sometimes a single composition might be considered appropriate for either a church or a mausoleum. So successful was Tiffany's business – and potential business – in designing, building, and furnishing decorative elements in mausoleums that in 1914 they published a booklet devoted exclusively to mausoleums.[19] That brochure not only tracked the history of memorializing individuals through monuments from ancient times to today, but extolled the firm's ability and excellence in each of the different branches of work. These comprised the design and construction of mausoleums, as well as the technical and engineering requirements. Such was their promotional

Fig. 134. Detail of mosaic work by Tiffany Studios in Fahnestock mausoleum, 1896. Photograph by Gavin Ashworth.

rhetoric that they aligned themselves with the development of the vogue for building private tombs in American cemeteries, saying "In the United States the great development in cemetery memorials along artistic lines may be considered as having had its inception when the department of out-of-door memorials became a branch of the Tiffany Studios."[20] Whether grand or modest, they designed and constructed mausoleums in a variety of revival styles – Egyptian, Byzantine, and Classical – all suggestive of the ancient practice of building monuments to the dead.

Tiffany Studios illustrated several interiors of mausoleums in the 1914 pamphlet, showcasing their work in marble fittings and mosaic. Elaborate mosaic work also became a mainstay of the firm's ecclesiastic work as seen at Woodlawn in the Margaret A. and Harris C. Fahnestock mausoleum designed by Peabody and Stearns in 1896 (Fig. 134). Presumably, Peabody and Stearns subcontracted the work to Tiffany Studios. Unfortunately, lack of documentation prevents our full understanding of the relationship between the Tiffany Studios and the architectural firm. One illustration in the published pamphlet (Fig. 135) featured the catacombs of richly veined marble, a Favrile glass mosaic dome, "specially designed Tiffany bronze lantern, a seat, and covers and rugs of special Tiffany fabrics."[21] Another included a Favrile glass window of a garden landscape, heralding the new natural landscape subject matter for which Tiffany Studios was best known. Another of their promotional pamphlets, *Memorial Windows*, promoted stained glass in mausoleums:

> The custom of erecting colored-glass windows in remembrance of the dead spread all over
> mediaeval Christendom – a usage that has been revived in our days, and has met with so
> much favor that all denominations are willing and glad to have their places of worship

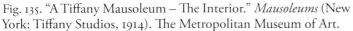

Fig. 135. "A Tiffany Mausoleum – The Interior." *Mausoleums* (New York: Tiffany Studios, 1914). The Metropolitan Museum of Art.

Fig. 136. Tiffany Glass and Decorating Company, Jeweled cross window for Colby mausoleum, ca. 1896. Photograph by Gavin Ashworth.

embellished with these works of art; believing it is not only right, but useful that those who have led exemplary lives and have finished the good fight should be remembered by those who are still in the battle; remembered not only by their friends and immediate relatives, but by all the people of the church.[22]

The company's *Mausoleums* pamphlet further promoted landscape windows saying: "The Light through a mausoleum window of Tiffany Favrile glass may reveal in all its true colors the cherished flower of a revered deceased member of a household; or, the same light may cause the iridescent Favrile glass to portray scenes of the natural life of the absent one; or, it may radiate pictures in the life of Christ, whom all good people like to emulate."[23] Similarly, at Woodlawn, multiple subjects ranging from crosses to figural scenes to verdant sunsets graced the mausoleums.

One of the earliest of the extant Tiffany windows is a small jewel-like rectangular window of a white opalescent cross framed by knots and surrounded by a wreath of purple and blue clematis (Fig. 136). The cross's background is bright white in the center of the window, drawing one in as if a holy light, surrounded by an elongated guioche pattern of multi-colored glass, which shades subtly from gold at the top to darker hues of blues and greens at the bottom. It bears the inscription "Simply to Thy Cross I Cling" and is signed by Tiffany Glass and Decorating Company, the firm's name until 1902 when it changed to Tiffany Studios. Indeed, such crosses and the use of glass jewels were characteristic of the early years of Tiffany's stained glass production and date prior to the turn of the century.[24] The textured jewel-like glass gives the window an unusual brilliance. The window graced the mausoleum commissioned by Anna Colby (1844-1898) following the death of her husband Charles Lewis Colby (1840-1896), who made his money in shipping, railroads, and mining.[25] The subject of the cross, the universal symbol of Christianity, was certainly appropriate given that Colby was highly religious, an ardent Baptist who worked for Baptist causes.[26]

Another early mausoleum window was on a lot purchased in 1899 by Sarah Josephine Wyckoff (1841-1921) in a mausoleum built to honor her husband Albert Wyckoff (1842-1899).[27] Wyckoff left his wife a considerable inheritance of about two million dollars at his untimely death. Framed by two opalescent columns with golden glass capitals and a canopy of golden scrolls with a heavenly crown in the center, the window is filled with three winged cherubim amidst lofty white clouds in a soft blue sky (Fig. 137). There is a softness about it that is the result of having a plate of glass over the entire window design. Such an image suggests the heavenly sky with the crown of Jesus in the heavens above. A similar subject was suggested by Tiffany Studios in three different watercolor presentations for a window commissioned by Miss Dorothy Blake for the Park Congregational Church in Grand Rapids, Michigan, as indicated in the inscriptions on their finished mats (Figs. 138, 139, 140). The winged cherubim in clouds, such as those escorting Christ to heaven in imagery of the Ascension, signify the flight of the spirit to heaven, and thus were appropriate in funerary depictions.

Fig. 137. Tiffany Glass and Decorating Company, Three cherubim window, for Wyckoff mausoleum, ca. 1899. Photograph by Gavin Ashworth.

No mausoleum better epitomizes the Tiffany Studios Ecclesiastical Department's ability to be a comprehensive firm – providing complete services from design concept, engineering, construction and materials, and interior embellishment – than the Currier mausoleum at Woodlawn (Fig. 141). In 1906 Jennie Currier (1844-1920) commissioned from the Studios the building of a classical mausoleum to memorialize her husband George C. Currier (1840-1905). The mausoleum was used to promote Tiffany Studios. They produced everything from the original design concept to completion of the final mausoleum, even furnishing a small model of the architectural structure, several views of which they published in their promotional pamphlet *Mausoleums* (Figs. 142, 143). They even published the completed Greek style mausoleum in its landscape setting at Woodlawn,

Figs. 138, 139, 140. Tiffany Studios, Design drawings of memorial windows with cherubim. The Metropolitan Museum of Art, Purchase, Walter Hoving and Julia T. Weld Gifts and Dodge Fund, 1967 (67.654.334), (67.654.335), (67.654.336). Image © The Metropolitan Museum of Art.

the name inscribed on the architrave visible in the photograph (Fig. 144). The stone was mined in the Tiffany Granite Quarry in Cohasset, Massachusetts. The interior was likewise fully designed and executed by Tiffany Studios Ecclesiastic Department, including the marble fittings and mosaic embellishment.

Tiffany Studios was also responsible for the leaded-glass window in the Currier mausoleum (Fig. 145), which was entitled *The Way to Emmaus*. Drawn from the Gospel of St. Luke, it shows Jesus Christ on the day of his Resurrection clothed in white robes tinged with pastel tones and greeted in supplication by two apostles. They entreat the traveler, whose identity is not yet revealed, to rest and stay, saying "Abide with us, for the day is far spent." In the description of a related window made in memory of Rev. Lewis Pyle Mercer for the Church of the New Jerusalem in Cincinnati dating to the year following the Currier window, the scene depicted is set in a rich landscape, and as described in a local newspaper, with "the effect of the lingering glow of the sun sinking beyond the distant hills and mellowing the haze of twilight."[28] Such a glowing description was no doubt furnished by the Tiffany Studios themselves, providing individualized yet formulaic press releases to myriad local newspapers who invariably printed the release verbatim. The subject was a popular one for memorial windows in churches for at least two decades.[29] Typically, the figures in the various versions of the subject are virtual duplicates of each other with minor changes to the gesture of the leading apostle. Based on the description, the design of the window is ascribed to Frederick Wilson (1858-1932), Tiffany's chief designer for figural windows. The differences lie in the backgrounds and the architectural treatment. The Currier window, for example, is a simple rectangular shape suited to the scale of the mausoleum, while those found in various church memorials are larger, often multi-lancet windows with decorative tracery above.

The largest and most complex Tiffany windows at Woodlawn decorate one of its grandest mau-

Figs. 142, 143. Model for Currier mausoleum. Tiffany Studios, *Mausoleums* (New York: Tiffany Studios, 1914). The Metropolitan Museum of Art.

Fig. 141. Currier mausoleum in Pine plot. Photograph by Charles D. Warren.

Fig. 144. Currier mausoleum at Woodlawn. Tiffany Studios, *Mausoleums* (New York: Tiffany Studios, 1914). The Metropolitan Museum of Art.

Fig. 145. Tiffany Studios, *Way to Emmaus* window for Currier mausoleum in Pine plot, c. 1906. Photograph by Lee Sandstead.

Fig. 146. Tiffany Studios, *Christ in Majesty* window for Harbeck mausoleum in Parkview plot, ca. 1917. Photograph by Gavin Ashworth.

Fig. 147. Tiffany Studios, *Christ in Majesty* window for Harbeck mausoleum in Parkview plot, ca. 1917. (detail) Photograph by Gavin Ashworth.

soleums. It is the one that Kate A. Harbeck (1859-1931) had built for her husband John H. Harbeck (c. 1840-1910). The impressive octagonal structure designed by Thomas Hastings and Theodore Blake houses a number of elaborate windows,[30] but its focal point is the three large Tiffany windows. The central window is a complex figural composition depicting Christ in Majesty, being crowned on his return to heaven having accomplished his mission on earth. As seen in this window, Christ is surrounded by angels and the elders, who are gathered around him to watch the ascent. Divided into nine sections, Christ occupies the central panel in white and pastel robes with blue clouds at his feet, stylized rays of the sun behind him, and the sky above a glowing pale yellow. In the panel directly below him are four angels playing musical instruments. At either side are the apostles, one holding a chalice, another holding a sword of flames, the whole scene then framed by clusters of winged cherubim. Such an ambitious window was most likely designed by Frederick Wilson, whose distinctive figural style can be seen especially vividly in the figures in the near foreground and the facial features of their painted faces (Figs. 146, 147). The British-trained Wilson, whose specialty was

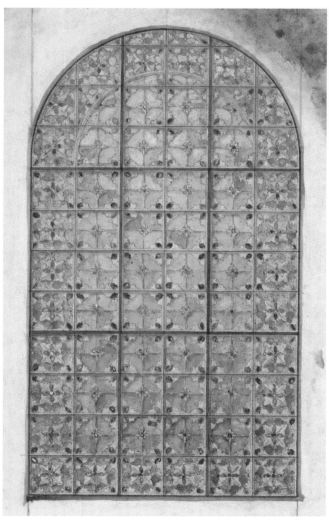

Fig. 148. Tiffany Studios, Window of Geometric design for Harbeck mausoleum in Parkview plot, ca. 1917. Photograph by Gavin Ashworth.

Fig. 149. Tiffany Studios, Design drawing of Geometric design for Harbeck mausoleum in Parkview plot, ca. 1917. The Metropolitan Museum of Art, Purchase, Walter Hoving and Julia T. Weld Gifts and Dodge Fund, 1967 (67.653.2). Image © The Metropolitan Museum of Art.

Figs. 150, 151, 152. Tiffany Studios, Three windows of life of Christ (Ascension, Nativity, Christ Preaching) for Cohan mausoleum in Butternut plot, ca. 1917. Photograph by Gavin Ashworth.

the depiction of religious figures, was one of the chief window designers for Tiffany Studios.

Two equally large windows in a geometric decorative design flank this central window (Fig. 148). It is an almost kaleidoscopic patterning of repeated geometric motifs that resemble paired butterflies with jewel-like centers, allowing plenty of light into the mausoleum, while at the same time giving that light a softness. The design drawing by Tiffany Studios for the simpler windows survives, and the final versions are remarkably close to the proposal submitted by Tiffany Studios for approval by Mrs. Harbeck (Fig. 149).

The Harbecks were a reclusive couple, who had houses in New York and in Boulder, Colorado. They built what was considered the grandest house in Boulder, which was graced by a window that may have been made by Tiffany's firm although no documentation to that effect is known.[31] He was a founding partner of a substantial warehousing empire in Brooklyn known as Harbeck Stores. He parlayed that fortune into in-

Fig. 153. Tiffany Studios, *Ascension* window for Miller mausoleum, ca. 1927. Photograph by Gavin Ashworth.

vestments in railroad stocks and other enterprises in Colorado. His wife, Kate, at the time of their marriage was a telegraph operator, but upon her husband's death she inherited Harbeck's enormous estate encompassing some seven million dollars. It was therefore fitting that she would build a mausoleum whose grandeur was commensurate with their fortune. Although Harbeck died in 1910, the mausoleum his wife built for him was not completed for another seventeen years. Mrs. Harbeck succumbed to death on New Year's Eve in 1930, due to a tragic accident having been crushed in the revolving door at the Plaza Hotel, is also interred in the mausoleum.

In 1917 George M. Cohan (1878-1942), the famous American entertainer, lyricist, and composer, built a mausoleum at Woodlawn for his sister Josephine Cohan Niblo who had died the previous year. His father, Jeremiah, along with his wife Helen Costigan Cohan, was a vaudeville entertainer from Rhode Island, died the following year and was also entombed in the mausoleum. George M. Cohan, his second wife, and his mother would later also be entombed in the mausoleum. Like the Currier mausoleum, the modestly scaled Gothic Revival style mausoleum was designed by Tiffany Studios, and fabricated by its Ecclesiastical Department in stone quarried from the Tiffany Granite Quarry in Cohasset, Massachusetts. Three windows designed by the Ecclesiastical Department were approved by Cohan,[32] and depict Jesus Christ at three different stages of his life in elliptical medallions in the style of thirteenth-century medallion windows on each of the three interior walls. In addition to the theme of the Ascension (Fig. 150), there is a nativity scene with Christ's birth and one of Christ preaching (Figs. 151, 152). The Ascension is portrayed with the figure of Christ, clad in long flowing white robes, ascending with arms upraised and flanked by two seraphim on each side. An intricate border of a geometric design in jewel tones of deep reds and blues surrounds the medallion. The windows were presumably installed in the Cohan mausoleum at the time of its construction. A vibrant border of brilliant red and blue variegated glass framed by emerald colored glass jewels conveys the sumptuous quality.

Tiffany Studios produced a virtual duplicate of the Cohan Ascension window a decade later at Woodlawn for the mausoleum Mildred Miller built for her husband Ralph E. Miller (d. 1923) (Fig. 153). Further evidence of the practice by the Studios of using a single design and even a cartoon for more than one commission is the discovery of a third window documented through a newspaper clipping in the extensive scrapbooks of the Studios in the collection of The Metropolitan Museum of Art. The article provides a glowing précis of the window as well as a picture, identical to both the Cohan and Miller windows, and noting its installation in a mausoleum in Poughkeepsie Rural Cemetery in 1926, for the late Reuben Borland, former president of the Alexander Smith and Sons Carpet Company.[33]

One of the most significant innovations in stained glass windows for mausoleums during the late nineteenth century was the introduction of landscapes as a subject. At Woodlawn, this new theme was represented by a number of windows. One of the more unusual was a series that the Tiffany Studios felt so proud of that they displayed them in their show rooms on Madison Avenue and 45th Street for ten days in May of 1910. They issued a press release for the series of seven windows that made up a continuous landscape with the Holy City in the central light created for the mausoleum that Robert Graves built to honor the death of his wife.[34] The windows were described as having the

Fig. 154. Tiffany Studios, Landscape window for Warner mausoleum in Lake plot, ca. 1925. Photograph by Gavin Ashworth.

Heavenly City in the central panel above a valley with a great abyss. The release provided an especially detailed evocation, all the more appreciated because so much of the original window is lost: "A range of mountains rises on either side of this valley until the summits are seen in the windows on each end. On the right they climb to a great height, with their snow-capped peaks, tinted with purple shades in the sky. Pine and dwarfed forest trees are growing in abundance on the slopes of the mountains."[35] The colors of the sunset were described as "gorgeous" with "beautiful blue, purple and golden tints." One of the more unusual features was the leading "placed diagonally across each window" that gave "the impression of looking through the grill out upon this glorious scene."[36] Regrettably, the Graves windows were presumably badly damaged at some point and were replaced with a modern schematic abstraction of the original mountain landscape.

While the Graves landscape was an ambitious multi-window panoramic landscape, a more typical landscape window by Tiffany Studios is the calm scenery fabricated for the mausoleum to memorialize Lucien Calvin Warner (1841-1925) (Fig. 154). Like many families represented at Woodlawn, Warner was a self-made man. He studied to be a doctor and practiced medicine in Cortlandville, New York, but soon began to focus on women's medical issues, lecturing and traveling around the country. Recognizing the health issues caused by the stiff restrictive corsets women wore, he went into partnership with his brother and developed a new safer and more flexible corset, called "Dr. Warner's Coraline Health Corsets." Such was their success, that the company grew exponentially, marketed its corsets around the country and abroad, and ultimately became the foundation of today's conglomerate, Warnaco. Warner's financial achievements placed him in the category of individuals able to memorialize their success with a lavish mausoleum at the prestigious Woodlawn cemetery, and to hire the most noted stained glass firm, Tiffany Studios, to provide the leaded glass window.

The Warner window's landscape composition is one favored for memorial windows in churches and mausoleums. It displays a strong tall tree in the right foreground with mountains in the distance and a placid lake in the middle ground. The golden light of the sky suggests a sunset view, appropriate as it was intended to memorialize an individual whose day is done. The window highlights the richness and variety of glass that Tiffany's studios developed and utilized to convey different pictorial effects. For example, the foliage of the tree is of a mottled green glass that highlights the coloristic properties of light filtered through leaves. This is further accentuated by the use of Tiffany's distinctive confetti glass whereby tiny flakes of glass are embedded into the flat glass, which achieves the look of fractured light through green foliage. In addition, the window is plated by adding a layer or more of panes of glass to the reverse of the window, thereby conveying a sense of recession and depth to the blue mountains in the distance.

There were many other landscape windows at Woodlawn. One, described in a *New York Times* clipping found in a Tiffany Studios scrapbook, was a "landscape art glass window" depicting a sunset scene for the mausoleum of Henry C. Ross.[37] Upon inspection, however, the mausoleum presents a gaping hole where the window should be. This is but one example of a leaded glass window, principally landscapes, looted from cemeteries like Woodlawn. This nefarious practice came to appalling light in 1999 during a much-publicized case exposing the practice, singling out one particular theft from a mausoleum at Salem Fields Cemetery in Brooklyn, New York.[38] Cemeteries, strapped for funds and unable to offer the necessary security, became easy targets for modern day tomb robbers intent on satisfying the demand for Tiffany windows. At Woodlawn alone, there are

Fig. 155. Edward Peck Sperry, *Angel before Cross.* Window in Rhinelander mausoleum in Fairview plot, c. 1907. Photograph by Gavin Ashworth.

at least twenty windows known to have been removed by theft during the late 1970s to the early 1990s. To make things more difficult, most stolen mausoleum windows are unable to be traced because, being private and largely hidden from view, they have not generally been adequately documented until very recently. Fortunately, Woodlawn has now photographed every window in their numerous mausoleums, which will provide invaluable documentation for the future.

Edward Peck Sperry (1850-1925), a stained glass artist who had previously worked for Tiffany Studios before setting up his own studio, was responsible for the opalescent glass window in the mausoleum honoring William Rhinelander (1825-1908) (Fig. 155). According to his obituary, Sperry had been in Tiffany's employ for about fifteen years beginning in about 1888 to about 1903, before going out on his own, following a brief stint with Gorham & Company. A New Haven native, he had studied for about two years at the Yale School of Fine Arts after entering in 1875, and continued his education with travels to Paris and Rome.[39] He was first listed as an artist in 1885, and the earliest mention of his work for Tiffany, then called the Tiffany Glass Company, occurs in 1887 for a chancel window.[40] He also produced four windows for St. James church in New York City in 1899. He taught stained glass at the New York School of Applied Design for Women at 200 West 23rd Street in 1899.[41] After his work with Tiffany, he worked for Gorham under contract to develop and supervise their new American Window Department from January 28, 1904 until July 20, 1906.[42] He then established the Church Glass & Decorating Company in 1906, with Caryl Coleman and Russell Foot, and was self-employed from 1911 until about 1921, when he retired due to ill health. His work is widespread in New York state and elsewhere.

Stylistically, Sperry's window can be distinguished from the work of Tiffany Studios in the boldness of the figure, and the background's high-keyed orange hue, lacking the soft and subtle tones often employed at Tiffany's. In addition, the cluster of flowers at the base of the cross is delineated by enamels painted on the surface of the glass, a technique that Tiffany eschewed wherever possible. Sperry worked in the opalescent mode of stained glass, but his window further departed from traditional Tiffany Studios work in the way that the glass is leaded together. Rather than the method preferred by Tiffany, whereby the leading was often minimized by employing copper foil and lead solder to join the window together, Sperry used the less labor-intensive method of thick lead came (strips) exclusively in this window, conferring a flatness and more decorative quality, attributable to the prominence of the black lead lines, even though he continued to incorporate integrally colored, folded, and textured glass similar to that used by Tiffany.

Another follower in the opalescent glass tradition of La Farge and Tiffany was the partnership of Oliver Speers Kimberly (1871-1956), who, like Sperry, had also worked in the window department at Tiffany Studios, and Francis Joseph Duffner (1860-1929). Their partnership was formed in 1906 and continued in operation only five years until 1911, when it folded due to financial difficulties, filing for bankruptcy on April 13, 1911.[43] The firm's reputation lies primarily in their lamps with leaded glass shades. The lack of documented Duffner and Kimberly windows and the short duration of the firm make the three executed for the mausoleum of John Martin at Woodlawn in 1908 all the more important. The subject of the central window is an Ascension (see Fig. 128). The window on the left, the most animated of the three, depicts John the Baptist in a landscape (Fig. 156). The stained

Fig. 156. Duffner and Kimberly, St. John the Baptist window for Martin mausoleum in Pine plot, 1908. Photograph by Gavin Ashworth.

Fig. 157. J. and R. Lamb Studios, Assumption of Blessed Virgin Mary window for Hillyer mausoleum in Filbert plot, 1911. Photograph by Gavin Ashworth.

glass artist J. Gordon Guthrie (1874-1961) worked as a designer for Duffner and Kimberly from 1906 until 1914, and it is possible that he may have had a role in this window.

One of Tiffany Studios biggest competitors in the ecclesiastical field was the firm of J. and R. Lamb, founded in 1857 by the two British-born Lamb brothers, Joseph and Richard. They were succeeded by the next generation, led by Charles Rollinson Lamb (1860-1942), following his father (Joseph's) death in 1898, and his younger brother Frederick Stymetz Lamb (1863-1928), who joined the firm after 1885, following artistic studies in both Paris and New York. From the inception, their firm, like Tiffany Studios, was a provider of all manner of decoration and they maintained throughout a particular focus on the ecclesiastic market. Their headquarters in New York City at 23, 24, and 27 Sixth Avenue were located nearby Tiffany's. According to their advertisements, they produced "metal, stained glass, mosaic, memorial brasses, memorial windows in modern or antique styles with historical or scriptural subjects"[44] Like Tiffany, they too published numerous trade catalogues, including *Memorial Chapels, Mausoleums and Monumental Work* in 1897.[45]

Clarence W. Hillyer (1869-1949) selected Lamb Studios when he had a mausoleum constructed in 1911, to memorialize his wife. The Lamb firm, sensitive to varying shifts in light, went so far as to discern the exact siting of the mausoleum so that they would know the direction and movement of the sun relative to their window, which they deemed "necessary ... in cutting the glass."[46] The window depicts *The Assumption of the Blessed Mary* into heaven (Fig. 157). Seen here as she is often depicted, the Virgin Mary is dressed in white with a blue robe around her and over her arm, with her head turned slightly toward heaven. She is surrounded by billowing clouds as she ascends at the end of her earthly life and is heralded into heaven by a pair of cherubim on the left and three on the right. The subject would suggest that the family who built the mausoleum was of the Catholic faith, as this would have been an atypical subject for a Protestant.

The mausoleum windows at Woodlawn Cemetery chronicle in microcosm the development of stained glass in America during the late nineteenth and early twentieth centuries. The windows, covering essentially four decades, mirror the techniques and styles that were concurrently designed for ecclesiastic and domestic spaces alike. The popularity of memorial windows for church interiors – and houses – no doubt influenced the inclusion of such windows in the design schemes for mausoleums, but also the use of stained glass was an effective way for families to make the connection between the temporal and the spiritual. Within these private funerary temples the brilliantly colored and filtered light of these devotional windows offset the often somber exteriors. As we have seen, like domestic spaces and church interiors of the period, mausoleum windows are but one component of an often complex decorative scheme that might include mosaic decoration, sculptural enhancements, decorative bronze work, carefully selected figured stone, and architectural details, all of which would be integrated into a unified whole. Likewise, the complexity of these decorative programs highlights the importance of collaboration between the stained glass designer and fabricator, the architect, and the patron.

The study of such a large number of stained glass windows at Woodlawn Cemetery has provided a unique opportunity for scholarly inquiry. The commitment made by Woodlawn to study, document, and preserve not only the architecture, sculpture, stained glass, and landscape, but also their documentation, through its collaboration with the Avery Architectural & Fine Arts Library at Columbia University, is unparalleled. It is hoped that this will set a standard toward which other cemeteries in New York and across the country can strive. For the most part, however, these mausoleum windows at Woodlawn stand as silent sentinels behind closed doors, unseen, unstudied and unpublished, much as the families who commissioned them wished them to be.

1. Patricia C. Pongracz, ed., *Louis C. Tiffany and the Art of Devotion* (New York: Museum of Biblical Art, 2013).

2. Lovett's body was also later transferred to the mausoleum.

3. Jean M. Farnsworth, Carmen R. Croce, Joseph F. Chorpenning, *Stained Glass in Catholic Philadelphia* (Philadelphia: Saint Joseph's University Press, 2002), 441.

4. See, for example, Nigel David Johnson, "Restoring the Stained Glass in Saint Michael's Church, Charleston," *Magazine Antiques* 168, no. 6 (December 2005): 84-91.

5. See Ivan Titus, "She Paints Antique Glass," *Mentor* (December 1927): 16-17.

6. Correspondence and specifications, Harkness mausoleum file, Woodlawn Cemetery Records, Drawings & Archives, Avery Architectural & Fine Arts Library, Columbia University (hereafter cited as Woodlawn Cemetery Records).

7. Ibid.

8. *Book of Common Prayer*.

9. Regarding Armstrong's work as an illustrator, see "Recent Work of Illustrators," *Brush and Pencil*, 10, no. 1 (April 1902): 27. See also *Ad Astra: Being Selections from the Divine Comedy of Dante* (New York: R.H. Russell, 1902), binding and decorations by Margaret Armstrong; illustrations by Helen Maitland Armstrong [Metropolitan Museum of Art, acc. No. 2012.128.8], with reserves of verse next to figural illustration.

10. I am most grateful to James L. Yarnall, former Director of the La Farge Catalogue Raisonné and Professor of Art History at Salve Regina University, Newport, Rhode Island, for generously sharing with me his research on this window.

11. "Miss Julia Lamont Dead," *New York Times*, Aug. 27, 1902. http://query.nytimes.com/mem/archive-free/pdf?res=F 40E13FF355414728DDDAE0A94D0405B828CF1D3

12. La Farge in Cecilia Waern. *La Farge: Artist and Writer* (London: Seeley, 1896), 54. Also available online at http:// catalog.hathitrust.org/Record/000369848

13. Yarnall, Entry for Lamont Family Mausoleum Window, manuscript for forthcoming Catalogue Raisonné of the Stained Glass of John La Farge.

14. The design of the mausoleum also had a La Farge connection in that it was one of the early designs by the architectural firm of Heins and La Farge, the latter partner, Christopher Grant La Farge, being John La Farge's son.

15. Information courtesy of James L. Yarnall.

16. James L. Yarnall, *John La Farge: a Biographical and Critical Study* (England: Ashgate Publishing, 2012), 264.

17. Frontispiece, salesman's sample books, Tiffany Glass Company, New York, undated (ca. 1885-1892), published in Alistair Duncan, *Louis C. Tiffany: The Garden Museum Collection* (Woodbridge, Suffolk, England: Antique Collector's Club, 2004), 100.

18. Tiffany Studios, *Memorials in Glass and Stone* (Baltimore, Md.: Printed by Munder Thomsen, 1913), [71], http:// libmma.contentdm.oclc.org/cdm/ref/collection/p16028coll5/id/1544

19. Tiffany Studios, *Mausoleums* (Tiffany Studios: New York, 1914), http://libmma.contentdm.oclc.org/cdm/ref/collection/p16028coll5/id/530

20. Ibid, [61].

21. Ibid, [57].

22. Tiffany Studios, *Memorial Windows* (Tiffany Studios: New York, 1896), [15]-[16], http://libmma.contentdm.oclc.org/cdm/ref/collection/p16028coll5/id/345

23. Tiffany Studios, *Mausoleums*, [61].

24. Several watercolor designs for windows of jeweled crosses appear in salesman's sample books of the Tiffany Glass Company, New York, undated (ca. 1885-1892), published in Alastair Duncan, *Louis C. Tiffany: The Garden Museum Collection* (Suffolk, England: Antique Collectors' Club, 2004), 112-113.

25. "Charles Lewis Colby Obituary," *New York Times*, February 28, 1896.

26. Ibid.

27. The architect for the mausoleum was Austin L. Gillespie. See "Two Imposing Granite Memorials," *Stone* 22, no. 3 (March 1901): 213.

28. "New Memorial Window Which Will Be Dedicated June 2," *Commercial Tribune* (Cincinnati), May 29, 1907, in Tiffany Studios Scrapbook, vol. 2, p.77, The American Wing, The Metropolitan Museum of Art (hereafter cited as Tiffany Studios Scrapbook).

29. See also the Rockwell memorial window in Pilgrim Congregational Church, Leominster, Massachusetts. "Church Memorial Window Dedicated," *Leominster Daily Enterprise*, June 9, 1924; and the Camp Memorial Window in St. Paul's Church, Milwaukee. "Memorial Window for St. Paul's, Milwaukee," *The Living Church*, October 2, 1926: 784.

30. Thomas Hastings of Carrère and Hastings worked in partnership with a number of younger architects in his office in the 1920's.

31. The floral window in the Harbeck's grand Colorado house is of opalescent glass, but without proper examination and documentation it is not possible to confirm its authorship.

32. Woodlawn Cemetery, General Conditions for Cohan mausoleum, Cohan mausoleum file, Woodlawn Cemetery Records.

33. "Medallion Window for Borland Mausoleum in Rural Cemetery," *Yonkers Herald*, December 3, 1926; in Tiffany Studios Scrapbook, vol. 4, p. 117. The window is described and illustrated.

34. Tiffany Studios Press Release, in Tiffany Studios Windows Scrapbook, vol. 2, p. 156.

35. Ibid.

36. Ibid.

37. Newspaper clipping "Briefer Mention," *New York Times*, April 8, 1928, in Tiffany Studios Scrapbook, vol. 4, p. 146.

38. See Benjamin Weiser, "Expert Charged in Sale of Tiffany Glass Stolen From Tomb," *New York Times*, May 19, 1999.

39. "Edward Peck Sperry, B. F. A., 1903," *Yale University Obituary Record of Graduates Deceased During the Year Ending July 1, 1926*, No. 85 (New Haven: Yale University, 1926), 280, http://mssa.library.yale.edu/obituary_record/1925_1952/1925-26.pdf

40. Architectural League Exhibition," *Art Amateur* 16 (January 1887): 37-38.

41. Advertisement, *Art Amateur*, June 1899: 41.

42. Paul F. Norton, "The 'American Window Department' of the Gorham Manufacturing Company, *Nineteenth Century* 23, no. 1 (2003): 13.

43. Randal J. Loy, "The Duffner & Kimberly Saint John Window, Kansas City (1911)" in "The Glorious Masterworks of Grace and Holy Trinity Cathedral, Kansas City, Missouri," http://www.leadedlamps.com/duffner/holytrinitywindowkansascity.com

44. *Low Art Tile Catalogue*, 1887, advertisement.

45. J & R. Lamb, *Memorial Chapels, Mausoleums and Monumental Work* (New York: J. & R. Lamb, 1897). Available on microfiche, Rakow Library, Corning Museum of Glass.

46. Correspondence J. & R. Lamb to Mr. Doolittle, Engineer, Woodlawn Cemetery, June 30, 1911, Hillyer Mausoleum files, Woodlawn Cemetery Records.

IMAGE SOURCES

Gavin Ashworth Photography, New York, NY

Avery Architectural & Fine Arts Library, Classics (rare books), Columbia University, New York, NY

Avery Architectural & Fine Arts Library, Drawings & Archives, Columbia University, New York, NY

Bronx Borough President's Office, Bronx, NY

Columbia University Libraries, New York, NY

Cornell University Library, Division of Rare and Manuscript Collections, Ithaca, NY

East Bloomfield Historical Society, East Bloomfield, NY

Frances Loeb Library, Harvard University Graduate School of Design, Cambridge, MA

The Green-Wood Cemetery, Brooklyn, NY

Library of Congress, Washington, DC

The Metropolitan Museum of Art, New York, NY

Museum of the City of New York, New York, NY

New-York Historical Society, New York, NY

Spring Grove Cemetery, Cincinnati, Ohio

Lee Sandstead, South Boston, VA

Charles D. Warren Architect, New York, NY

Environmental Design Archives, University of California, Berkeley, CA

Westerly Public Library & Wilcox Park, Westerly, Rhode Island

CONTRIBUTORS

ANDREW SCOTT DOLKART is a Professor of Historic Preservation and the Director of the Historic Preservation Program at the Columbia University School of Architecture, Planning and Preservation. He is the author of three award-winning books: *Morningside Heights: A History of Its Architecture and Development; Biography of a Tenement House in New York City: An Architectural History of 97 Orchard Street;* and *The Row House Reborn: Architecture and Neighborhoods in New York City, 1908-1929,* the 2012 winner of the Society of Architectural Historians' Antoinette Forrester Downing Award. He is currently working on a book examining the architecture and development of New York's Garment District.

CAROLE ANN FABIAN is Director, Avery Architectural & Fine Arts Library where she oversees its research and special collections, and its programs for research, teaching and exhibition. Her work, publications, and presentations focus on community collaborations that support the management and use of large scale architectural archives – such as the recent co-acquisition of the Frank Lloyd Wright Foundation Archives with The Museum of Modern Art – and on development of technical and policy frameworks for born-digital architectural archives.

ALICE COONEY FRELINGHUYSEN is the Anthony W. and Lulu C. Wang Curator of American Decorative Arts at The Metropolitan Museum of Art in New York. She has published widely and curated numerous exhibitions on American ceramics and glass, especially the work of Louis Comfort Tiffany, as well as late nineteenth-century American furniture and patronage. Ms. Frelinghuysen is currently working on a book on the Robert A. Ellison Jr. Collection of American Art Pottery.

CYNTHIA MILLS was a specialist in nineteenth-century sculpture. She served as the Executive Editor of *American Art* at the Smithsonian American Art Museum (SAAM), and coordinator of SAAM's fellowship program. She retired in 2011 and was named a Smithsonian Historian Emeritus. She lectured widely in the US and abroad, and published numerous papers and essay collections. Her book *Beyond Grief: Sculpture and Wonder in the Gilded Age Cemetery* was published posthumously in September, 2014.

SUSAN OLSEN is the Director of Historical Services for the Woodlawn Cemetery. Her experience is in the field of historical museums and properties having held the positions of Chief of the Bureau of Historical Museum with the Florida Department of State, Director of Woodlawn Plantation and Frank Lloyd Wright's Pope Leighey House, a National Trust site, and Director of the Key West Art and Historical Society.

JANET PARKS is Curator of Drawings & Archives at the Avery Architectural & Fine Arts Library where she has overseen collections documenting the history of 19th and 20th century American architecture since 1978. She has curated and published catalogs for numerous exhibitions including *The Troubled Search: The Work of Max Abramovitz, Mastering McKim's Plan: Columbia's First Century on Morningside Heights,* and *The Old World Builds the New: the Guastavino Company and the Technology of the Catalan Vault, 1885-1962.*

CHARLES D. WARREN is an architect whose practice is based in Manhattan. He is co-author of *Carrère & Hastings Architects* and author of introductory essays for new editions of *The Architecture of Charles A. Platt* and John Nolen's classic *New Towns for Old.*

INDEX

Page numbers in **bold** indicate illustrations.

OVSZ 718 SYLV
Sylvan cemetery :

FEB 2 6 2019

SET IN GARAMOND, SCHNEIDLER INITIALS, AND DELPHIAN TYPES.

PRINTED ON GALLERIE SILK PAPER.

DESIGNED BY JERRY KELLY.

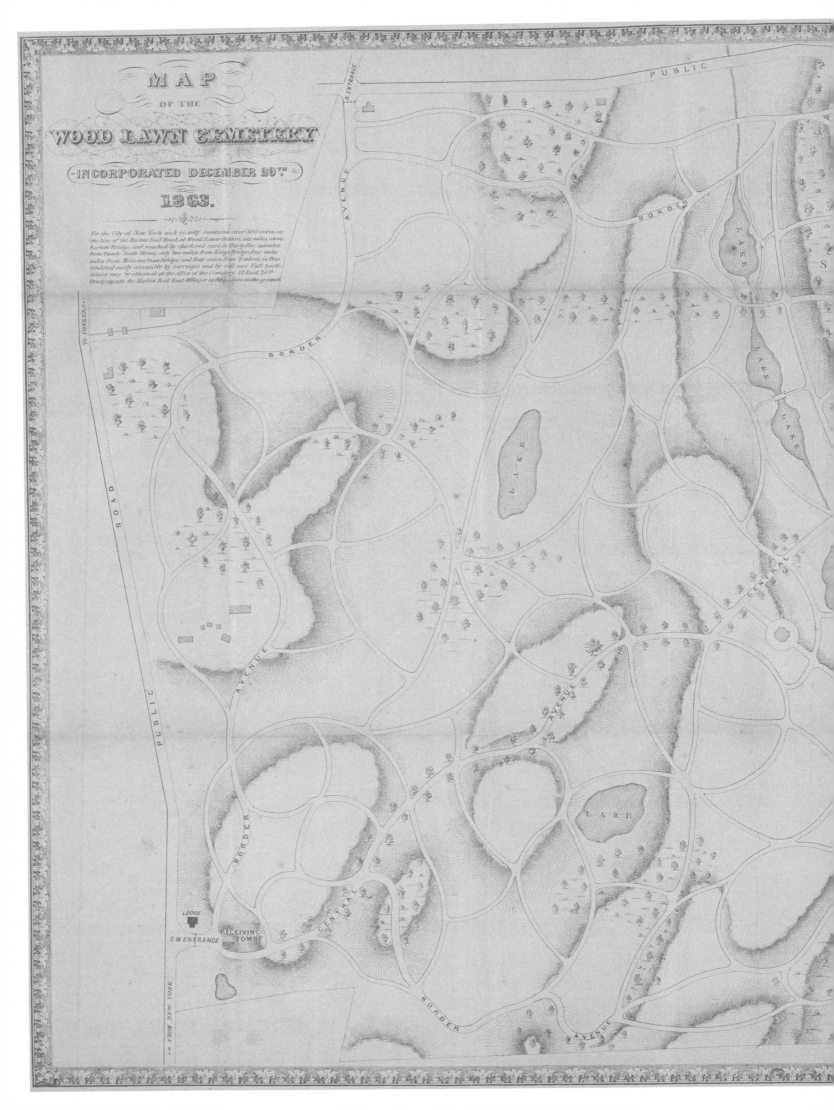

MAP
OF THE
WOOD LAWN CEMETERY
INCORPORATED DECEMBER 29TH
1863.

For the City of New York and vicinity, contains over 300 acres, on the line of the Harlem Rail Road, at Wood Lawn Station, six miles above Harlem Bridge, and reached by chartered cars in thirty-five minutes from Twenty-Sixth Street, only two miles from Kings Bridge, four miles from McGown's Dam Bridge, and four miles from Yonkers, is thus rendered easily accessible by carriages and by rail cars. Full particulars may be obtained at the office of the Cemetery, 52 East 26th Street, (opposite the Harlem Rail Road Office,) or at the Lodges on the grounds.

LODGE

S.W. ENTRANCE

RECEIVING TOMB